KT-116-964

First Class

compiled by
Donald W Stewart

Pop music rounds by
Philip Whitfield Aikman

BBC BOOKS

Published by BBC Books
A division of BBC Enterprises Ltd
Woodlands, 80 Wood Lane, London, W12 0TT

First published 1988
© British Broadcasting Corporation 1988

ISBN 0 563 20664 0

Photoset by Wilmaset
Birkenhead, Wirral
Printed in Great Britain by
Richard Clay Ltd, Bungay, Suffolk

BBC QUIZBOOKS
FIRST CLASS

CONTENTS

FOREWORD

It really has been tremendous fun recording the first three series of *First Class* at the BBC in Glasgow, but I can't tell you how glad I am to be the one *asking* the questions rather than trying to answer them. I'm constantly amazed not only at the contestants' knowledge on subjects as diverse as Greek mythology and the Beastie Boys, but also at the speed with which they recall all the facts.

And you know, answering questions as you sit relaxed at home in front of the box waiting for your mum or dad to cook dinner is an entirely different matter from being under the spotlight. Just picture it. You're on telly for the first time in your life, there's a live studio audience to contend with, all your family and friends are watching so you dread making a fool of yourself, and you desperately want to beat the other school. The pressure is really on, so it's no wonder that contestants sometimes get a little buzzer-happy when their brains run ahead of their tongues. One young lad has my eternal sympathy as he, knowing that the heat would be decided on the final question, beat everyone to the buzzer and announced to millions of people that the first name of the painter Van Gogh was Edward. I knew exactly how he felt because many years previously, as a proud member of the Belle Vale Primary School quiz team, I'd pronounced with complete certainty to all the assembled family and friends in the local library that the Milk Race took place on cows. I felt an udder failure and it took me years and much teasing to get over that one.

I must confess to being equally hopeless at the video arcade games. If it had been left to me space invaders would have taken us over ten years ago. Oops, I'm showing my age. Try as I might to impress with my lightning reflexes on Atari 720 or Hypersport, my efforts are always rewarded by the message 'You failed to qualify' flashing on the screen for all to see.

But there is one question I can definitely answer; why is Eugene called Eugene? Simple. The computer whizz kid who originally programmed our BBC Micro is called Eugene Crozier. Anyway, can you think of a better name?

If you have enjoyed watching the programme and you suspect that your school could do better than some of our teams, why not get one of your teachers to drop a line to the BBC at Queen Margaret Drive in Glasgow? You never know, *you* could be our First Class of 1989.

Debbie Greenwood

How to play *First Class*

It's easy to create the friendly rivalry of *First Class* away from the television studio and in your home, club or school. Some of the questions in this book have been asked during *First Class* on BBC1, but a large number have been written specially by the same people who provide the questions Debbie Greenwood uses in the studio.

In the programme itself, two teams compete to answer the most questions correctly – and fastest on the bell or buzzer. Some rounds are open to everyone; others are for one player only, to answer in their own time (within reason!).

Using this book, you can adopt whichever of these styles you wish. If four or more contestants are taking part, it's a good idea to vary the rules between 'open' and 'individual' answering from round to round. That can make the quiz even more entertaining because it varies the pace, and allows people to shine who may not always be first to reply but who nonetheless have a good general knowledge.

Another way to play is to set a time limit so that it's up to the individual or team to answer as many questions as they can in, say, two minutes.

If you're on your own you can set yourself a 'target' of, perhaps, eight questions correct out of every twelve – again possibly to a time limit.

It's two points for a correct answer, with one point for a very near miss.

Whatever you do, this book is designed to help you test your own general knowledge and that of your friends . . . but most of all to have fun doing so. 'Good fun' is the overwhelming verdict of contestants and audience alike, and here are almost 1,200 questions for you to experience that for yourself!

Donald W Stewart

GAME ONE

1 In the 1830s, which scientist made journeys of discovery aboard HMS *Beagle*?

2 In the game of Scrabble, which of these letters has the highest value – H, V or K?

3 In the cartoon series *Dogtanian and the Three Muskehounds*, what is the name of Dogtanian's faithful horse?

4 Which star of Buck's Fizz co-presented *The Saturday Picture Show* on television?

5 Who was the leader of Little John and Friar Tuck?

6 What can travel to the far side of the world, yet stay in its own corner?

7 What is the Italian word for 'writing' that has come to be associated with slogans on walls?

8 On which objects in everyday use would you see the letters D G REG F D?

9 Where is the Treasury Bench?

10 Which woollen hat sounds like a fruit?

11 Cob, cottage, Vienna and French stick are all types of what?

12 To make new words, which single three-letter word can you place in front of: office, room, kite and junction?

GAME ONE   POP MUSIC (1)

1   What is the name of the apartment building in New York in which John Lennon lived and outside which he was killed?

2   Name the film that launched Hazel O'Connor's singing career.

3   Name the hit single for which Captain Kirk was responsible in the summer of 1987.

4   Who is the only artist to have won the Eurovision Song Contest twice?

5   Who was involved with the USSR in June 1986?

6   Which group were left breathless in November 1986?

7. What did Radio One celebrate in September 1987?

8   In January 1983, what chart replaced the BMRB chart used by the BBC to compile each week's list of hit singles?

9   What is the title of the theme music to the TV series *M.A.S.H*?

10 How high in the charts did the *M.A.S.H.* theme reach?

11 Elvis Costello had two minor hits in 1983 and 1984 under another name. What was that other name?

12 From where do UB40 take their name?

1 In which area of British working life was there a so-called 'Big Bang' in October 1986?

2 To which country did Mrs Thatcher travel for a Commonwealth Prime Ministers' conference in the autumn of 1987?

3 Which coin stopped being legal tender at the end of 1984?

4 Norman Willis has been in the headlines as general secretary of a major national organisation. What is the name of the organisation?

5 In 1986, who became the Government's Cabinet Minister for Education and Science?

6 Who was born at St Mary's Hospital in Paddington on 15 September 1984?

7 In which field did David and Elizabeth Emmanuel reach the top during the 1980s?

8 What did Mrs Jennifer Guinness have in common with Patty Hearst and Shergar?

9 Which British political leader of the 1980s has a surname that begins and ends with the same letter?

10 In which country did the Prince and Princess of Wales watch a display of Sumo wrestling in May 1986?

11 In which country has the township of Soweto been the scene of rioting in recent years?

12 Which wizard appeared on a special issue 17-pence stamp in September 1985?

GAME ONE   MOVIES

1 In which film did furry little creatures called the Ewoks first appear?

2 In 1985, the Ewoks starred in their own adventure film. What was its title?

3 In which full-length Disney cartoon do sisters called Anastasia and Drizella appear?

4 Who wrote the Oscar-winning musical score for *Out of Africa*?

5 Which major Film Festival awards a top prize called the 'Golden Palm'?

6 In May 1986, which British film won that 'Golden Palm'?

7 Which film was set in America's gangland of the 1930s and starred Jodie Foster with an all-child cast?

8 The film *Ring of Bright Water* told the story of Mij. What kind of animal was he?

9 Which animal featured in the trademark of the great Metro-Goldwyn-Mayer film studio?

10 In which musical film will you hear the song 'Feed the Birds'?

11 'The Cuckoo Song' was linked with which great cinema comedians?

12 Which number is missing from this film title: — *Days at Peking*?

GAME ONE   SPORTS AND GAMES

1   What is the first name of athlete Daley Thompson? Is it Francis, David or Lawrence?

2   Which top English football team are nicknamed 'The Gunners'?

3   Which county cricket club has its headquarters at the Kennington Oval?

4   Which international football competition was known as the Nations Cup until 1960?

5   In which city were the first 'modern' Olympics held in 1896?

6   For which country has the great athlete Marita Koch been a star?

7   Is football's World Cup held every three, four or five years?

8   A world championship was held for the first time at Coxheath in 1968. Was it ludo, wrestling or custard pie throwing?

9   In which sport might you use rings, the side horse or the balance beam?

10   What do you need to play the games Boss Out, Ring Taw and Bombers?

11   When would you use an Eskimo roll? Would it be when wrestling, canoeing, or ice skating?

12   In boxing, which is heavier – a middleweight or a welterweight?

1   Which group did a highly successful cover of 'Only you' by Yazoo?

2   What is Boy George's middle name?

3   'Move over darling' was a hit for Doris Day in 1964. Who took it to the top ten in December 1983?

4   Name the lead singer of the early 1980s group Soft Cell.

5   What are the initials of the New York based TV station that plays continuous pop videos?

6   Name the capital city of the country that The Human League were singing about in 1984.

7   Which hours of the day link Dolly Parton and Sheena Easton?

8   Which Ultravox hit had biblical connections?

9   Name the Scottish female singer who sang on Mike Oldfield's singles 'Moonlight shadow' and 'To France'.

10 Orchestral Manoeuvres in the Dark had a hit with the song 'Enola Gay'. What was the original *Enola Gay*?

11 From which country does the singer Sade come?

12 Which chemical element features in the pop group Queen?

1   Which European language is the main language of Brazil?

2   What is a Camberwell Beauty?

3   What kind of creature is a red-bellied tamarin?

4   We know what a skunk is – but what kind of creature is a skink?

5   Which sea is connected to the Mediterranean by the Bosporus, and is bounded by Turkey, Bulgaria, Romania and the Soviet Union?

6   Which country is 'home' to the emu?

7   In economics, what do the initials GNP stand for?

8   Where on a horse's body would you find the part known as the coronet? – Would it be on its foot, its chest or its head?

9   In the book by Roald Dahl, who was 'Champion of the World'?

10 In the children's rhyme, who 'went to bed with his trousers on . . . one shoe off, and the other shoe on'?

11 A tea strainer is 2.5 cm deep and has a diameter of 5 cm. How many fluid ounces of tea will it hold?

12 What is the popular name for latitude 66 degrees, 33 minutes North?

GAME TWO

1 If you list the Books of the New Testament in alphabetical order, which is first? ✓

2 Subtract the year of Magna Carta from the year of the Battle of Waterloo, and what number are you left with?

3 Which is the largest marsupial animal?

4 What is the name of Moscow's top ballet theatre company, set up in 1780?

5 Who created Mrs Tittlemouse and Jemima Puddle-Duck?

6 What is monosodium glutamate generally used for?

7 A horse is facing north-east. In which direction is its tail pointing?

8 On television, who portrays Vince Prince, the eternal Teddy Boy?

9 Which well-known walkway stretches 270 miles from Edale to Kirk Yetholm?

10 If a pianist plays eight bars of a waltz, how many beats of music has he played? ✓

11 In their natural habitat, walruses are found only in the Antarctic. True or false?

12 Who was Lindlow Man?

GAME TWO POP MUSIC (1)

1 What is Paul McCartney's first name?

2 The Flying Pickets perform a particular type of singing. What is it called?

3 Susanne Sulley and Joanne Catherall are the female members of which group?

4 Who was 'Solid' at number three in January 1985?

5 What is the name of the computer-generated character who presented pop video shows on Channel 4?

6 Name the Dutch producer who was behind the Starsound hits of 1981 and 1982.

7 What is the title of Supertramp's autumn 1987 album?

8 Which number links George Orwell with the group the Eurythmics?

9 Which army person was 'trapped' at number three in October 1985?

10 If the Weather Girls had held their umbrellas upside down in March 1984, what would they have caught?

11 'Punk' was originally an Elizabethan word meaning what?

12 Where does the name of the group Buck's Fizz come from?

1   In which month of 1987 was Britain's General Election held?

2   Which famous broadcaster became a Doctor of Law of Leeds University in 1986, causing newspapers to comment: 'How's about that, then'?

3   In British politics, which party partnered the Social Democratic Party to form the Alliance?

4   In the spring of 1986, why were people in parts of Britain advised not to drink rain water?

5   In which year did the old sixpenny (or $2\frac{1}{2}$ p) coin cease to be legal tender in Britain?

6   Which pop star did the Queen make an honorary knight in the summer of 1986?

7   Which medicine was withdrawn from use in the summer of 1986 because of fears that it might cause a rare disease called Reye's Syndrome?

8   Of which European country did Kurt Waldheim become president in 1986?

9   After which natural disaster of 1985 did opera singer Placido Domingo organise a world-wide relief fund?

10 The nine hundredth anniversary of a book was celebrated in 1986. Which book?

11 Of which English city was Derek Hatton a controversial deputy council leader during the 1980s?

12 Terry Waite made several overseas journeys in the 1980s as a special envoy on behalf of whom?

GAME TWO   MOVIES

1   Which great star of cinema tap dance, perhaps best known for his partnership with Ginger Rogers, died in 1987?

2   Which star of Western films was nicknamed 'Duke'?

3   Which city is missing from the title of this Robert Greenhut and Woody Allen film: *The Purple Rose of – – – – –*?

4   Which category of British Academy Award was won by Rosanna Arquette for her part in *Desperately Seeking Susan*?

5   What is the popular name for the main awards of the American Academy of Motion Picture Arts and Sciences?

6   Who directed the Oscar-winning film *Out of Africa*?

7   Which Disney film gave us the 'Siamese Cat Song'?

8   What was Walt Disney's middle name? Was it Earl, Endell or Elias?

9   In which classic children's film do we meet a dog called Toto and a girl named Dorothy?

10   Who says 'What's up, Doc'?

11   Which series of comedies went 'Up the Khyber', 'Up the Jungle' and 'At Your Convenience'?

12   Which American comedian provided the voice of Bernard, the janitor in Disney's *The Rescuers*?

1   If you're learning karate, are you more advanced if you are graded as a brown belt or as a white belt?

2   This football team has been nicknamed 'the Rams', and they play home games at the Baseball Ground. Who are they?

3   Which sport uses the Queensberry Rules?

4   In a standard set of twenty-eight dominoes, how many 'doubles' are there?

5   In which sport might you try to win the Ryder Cup?

6   In which sport did Mark Spitz win seven gold medals at the 1972 Olympics?

7   To the nearest mile, how long is the course of the Oxford and Cambridge University Boat Race?

8   At which boxing weight has Marvin Hagler won the world title?

9   Who won the Open Golf Championship in Britain in 1987?

10 If you watched a Five Nations Championship match at Murrayfield, what would the sport be?

11 In which sport have Karen Barber and Nicky Slater reached the top?

12 At the Los Angeles Olympics in 1984, who was involved in a spectacular collision with Mary Decker Slaney?

GAME TWO   POP MUSIC (2)

1   In 1985, Billy Connolly had a hit with the theme to a children's TV comedy show. What was the name of the show?

2   Who wrote and performed the theme music for the TV show *Miami Vice*?

3   In the UK, how many albums have to be sold before a platinum disc is awarded? ✓

4   Who had a hit with 2 De's, 3 Do's and 3 Da's?

5   Who sang 'It's 'orrible being in love when you're 8½'?

6   Which group went 'back to their roots' in May 1981?

7   What is the real name of Kid Creole of Kid Creole and the Coconuts?

8   Who tooted twice in June 1985?

9   Who couldn't finish his reading in October 1985?

10   Which British group won the 1981 Eurovision Song Contest?

11   Who did Bananarama team up with to have a 1982 hit called 'Really saying something'?

12   Can you name the last chart entry in the *Guinness Book of Hit Singles*?

GAME TWO   GENERAL KNOWLEDGE (2)

1 Which gas is known as marsh gas, and is also the main ingredient of so-called 'natural gas'?

2 In which country is the holy city of Mecca?

3 Which of these cities lies furthest north: Moscow, Manchester or New York?

4 Which two main London railway stations have the word 'Cross' in their names?

5 What would you do with a Sopwith Camel – fly it, feed it or wear it?

6 On which British island group is the town of Kirkwall?

7 Which group of islands off Britain includes Tresco, St Agnes and St Mary's?

8 In anatomy, what is the usual name for the fluid part of our blood that contains blood cells?

9 What is the formal name for the science the television weathermen use in their job?

10 What is metrology?

11 Which bird was once called the 'Indian hen'?

12 In which month of the year do Americans hold their Thanksgiving day?

GAME THREE

1 On a restaurant menu, what would the eggs of the sturgeon fish be called?

2 Who wrote a poem about 'The Lady of Shallot', first published in 1832?

3 Which traditional song has 'Parsley, sage, rosemary and thyme' as its second line?

4 Who was our monarch during World War Two?

5 Who reigned over us when Admiral Nelson won the Battle of Trafalgar?

6 Do we have more bones in our arms or in our legs – or the same in each?

7 What nationality was the composer Schubert?

8 In a mediaeval suit of armour, which part of the body was covered by the beaver?

9 In chemistry, which element took its name from the Greek for 'violet-coloured'?

10 If he's an ENT specialist, which parts of you would a doctor examine?

11 On traffic lights, which signal follows red on its own?

12 Which Canadian territory lies north of British Columbia and west of the North-West Territories?

GAME THREE   POP MUSIC (1)

1   Which UK promoter worked with Bob Geldof on promoting Live Aid?

2   Who drummed in both Wembley and Philadelphia on 13 July 1985?

3   Who sang 'Hold me' with BA Robertson in October 1981?

4   Name Julio Iglesias' only number one UK hit.

5   Name Duran Duran's keyboard player.

6   In what was Simon Le Bon travelling when he was nearly killed in 1985?

7   Which East European lady did Elton John take to number three in the charts of 1985?

8   What are the Christian names of the members of the group Bananarama?

9   Who had a hit with '99 red balloons' in February 1984?

10   Who was up 'Gasoline Alley' in 1983?

11   In March 1986, the comedy team The Young Ones reached number one in a remake of a song with the original artist. Who is he?

12   Name the lead singer with The Pretenders.

GAME THREE   NEWS OF THE '80s

1   Which popular Greek singer was held hostage during an airliner hijacking in the Middle East in 1985?

2   In which year did the Falklands conflict take place between Britain and Argentina?

3   What name did the Argentinians give to the Falkland Islands?

4   In the 1980s, which local tax did the Government announce they wanted to replace with a 'community charge'?

5   Which industry, in the news over disputes during the 1980s, has trade union members in the NUJ, the NGA and SOGAT?

6   In May 1986, what did the barn owl and pine marten have in common with the wildcat and the natterjack toad?

7   During 1986, Mrs Thatcher had talks with Prime Minister Shimon Peres. Of which country is he Prime Minister?

8   Which flower did the Labour Party adopt as its symbol before the General Election in 1987?

9   Who made a British bid for the Trans-Atlantic water speed crossing in June 1986?   ✓

10   By which means of transport did that same man make another Atlantic crossing in 1987 in search of another record?

11   Which 'farewell' made the headlines at Wembley Stadium on 28 June 1986?

12   In 1981, the Queen opened a bridge heralded as the longest single-span suspension bridge in the world. Which British estuary does it span?

1 Which author's stories were retold in the film *All Creatures Great and Small*, starring Simon Ward?

2 In the film *Romancing the Stone*, what was the name of the novelist played by Kathleen Turner?

3 In the 1986 film about Biggles, who played the title role?

4 Who starred with Bruce Willis in *Blind Date*?

5 In the title of the Western film, who is the partner of the 'Sundance Kid'?

6 Bob Hoskins won a 'best actor' award at the 1986 Cannes Film Festival for his part in which film?

7 Which film 'Academy' starred Steve Guttenberg and Kim Cattrall?

8 Complete the title of the 1987 Spielberg cartoon *The American* . . .

9 In *Bambi*, what kind of creature was Flower?   √

10 Which pop star played the lead in the film *Ziggy Stardust and the Spiders from Mars*?

11 Who is the star of *Trading Places* who has also made his name in *Beverly Hills Cop* pictures?

12 Add together the numbers of brides and brothers in the title of the classic musical starring Howard Keel, and which number should you have?   √

GAME THREE   SPORTS AND GAMES

1   In which English city will you find Anfield and Goodison Park football grounds?

2   Which city is 'home' to the football clubs of Hearts and Hibs?

3   At how many Olympic Games has Daley Thompson won gold in the decathlon?

4   In basketball, how many players can be on court at any one time for each team?

5   What was it that Matthew Webb was first to do in August of 1875, taking 21 hours and 45 minutes to finish?

6   Which sport has the CTC encouraged over the years?

7   In which game could you come across the Paris Opening and the Sicilian Defence?

8   In which sport did Boomerang help Eddie Macken?

9   In which sport has Franz Klammer gone from the top to the bottom faster than anyone else?

10   Where would you find Valentine's Brook, the Chair and Beecher's Brook?

11   In which year were the Commonwealth Games last held?

12   When the Commonwealth Games were last held in Edinburgh, who won the men's 800 metres gold medal?

GAME THREE POP MUSIC (2)

1 Who was quoting Shakespeare in May 1980?

2 Which artist had a hit in 1982 with the old Supremes' song 'You can't hurry love'?

3 Real Madrid had a reserve goalkeeper who became a singer. Name him.

4 In November 1986, 'Don't give up' was a hit for Peter Gabriel and which other singer?

5 What is Tina Turner's real name?

6 Who was 'Walking on sunshine' in May 1985?

7 Who founded Tamla Motown records?

8 Who was on auto-pilot in February 1983?

9 Who did Annie Lennox of the Eurythmics sing with on the hit single 'Sisters are doing it for themselves'?

10 Name Bruce Springsteen's number one album of October 1987.

11 Why was Duran Duran's video 'Girls on film' banned?

12 Who shot and killed the singer Marvin Gaye?

1 Which geometric figure is also a musical instrument?

2 In area, which is the second largest State of Australia?

3 In a mediaeval church, what shape would you expect a 'rose window' to be?

4 If you enjoy tintinnabulation, what is your hobby?

5 Which part of your body is also a fish?

6 The character of Portia is to be found in Shakespeare's play *Julius Caesar*. True or false?

7 Who wrote the book *Tales of a Fourth Grade Nothing*?

8 If a circular birthday cake is cut into eight equal slices, how many degrees of the circumference do I remove with three slices?

9 Who wrote the novel *Kane and Abel*, televised in June 1986?

10 Which number gives you 2,500 when you multiply it by itself?

11 In legend, what kind of creatures were the Centaurs?

12 Last century, in which city did the 'Peterloo Massacre' happen?

GAME FOUR

GAME FOUR   GENERAL KNOWLEDGE (1)

1   On television, who is the human friend of Gordon the Gopher?

2   Luxembourg, West Germany, Austria and Belgium: three of these countries have flags with horizontal stripes. Which is the odd one out?

3   On television in the autumn of 1986, whose assistant was played by Bonnie Langford?

4   Which country built the great Aswan dam in 1970?

5   In which field of achievement did Chris Bonington make his name?

6   In music, how many quavers equal three minims?

7   Which ballet features a girl called Clara, the Kingdom of Sweets and a Flower Waltz?

8   Which day of the year lasts only twenty-three hours? ✓

9   If March the first is a Saturday, on which day of the week is the following first of April?

10   Which single five-letter word goes before all these words: Derby, prince and jewels?

11   In which sea does Cuba lie?   ✓

12   What is a diamond-back? Is it a rattle-snake, a turtle, or a moth?

GAME FOUR   POP MUSIC (1)

1   What is the full title of the 1983 Duran Duran album which begins with the number seven?

2   Who did Phil Collins replace as lead singer with Genesis?

3   What did Falco ask Mozart to do in 1986?

4   Who enjoyed a rainy night in 1981?

5   Who wrote a song about Edinburgh's High Street or 'Royal Mile'?

6   Who was travelling 2000 miles in November 1983?

7   In which year was 'Living Doll' originally a hit for Cliff Richard?

8   Which group did a spoof cover version of Queen's 'Bohemian Rhapsody' in October 1987?

9   What are the surnames of the two Pet Shop Boys?

10   Where was Michael Jackson born?

11   Name Michael Jackson's famous producer.

12   What kind of music is played by Bob Marley and Peter Tosh?

1   In September 1986, who did Mark Curry replace as a *Blue Peter* television presenter?

2   Britain's National Garden Festival of 1988 is in Glasgow. Where did the last National Garden Festival before that take place?

3   Who resigned as leader of the Labour Party in 1983?

4   In 1984, why was Bruce McCandless in the headlines?

5   In which country did President Tito die in 1980?

6   Who became the President of France in 1981?

7   Which church was the scene of the wedding of the Prince and Princess of Wales?

8   In May 1986, who took over from Mike Read as presenter of Radio One's breakfast show?

9   Which two countries joined the European Economic Community in 1986?

10   In which British stadium was the big 'Live Aid' concert held in July 1985?

11   In the autumn of 1987, for which creature in Britain did Adrian Shine organise a big hunt (although he was later reported as saying the creature was a 'media myth')?

12   To which historic encounter did the European 'Giotto' spacecraft travel in March 1986?

GAME FOUR   MOVIES

1   Which film, released in 1986, was the sequel to *Romancing the Stone*?

2   Who is the famous father of film star Michael Douglas?

3   Who was the star of *King Solomon's Mines*, on our cinema screens in 1986?

4   Which Disney cartoon film was re-issued in 1987 to mark its 50th birthday?

5   What is the surname of famous film star father and daughter Ryan and Tatum?

6   Which place name completes the title of the popular 1986 film that began *Down and Out in. . .*?

7   In 1985, F. Murray Abrahams won an Oscar as best actor for his performance in which film?

8   Which top picture in 1981 told the story of rivalry between two athletes called Harold Abrahams and Eric Liddell?

9   What was the name of the zany police force which starred in silent films made by Mack Sennett for the Keystone Film Company?

10   What was the first name of the governess played by Julie Andrews in *The Sound of Music*?

11   Which great film star, who died in 1987, had a number one hit in Britain with 'Wand'rin' Star'?

12   From which film did 'Wand'rin' Star' come?

1 In May 1985, which countries competed for the first time for the Rous Trophy?

2 In which United Kingdom city is a national football cup final played at Windsor Park?

3 Which boxer from Louisville called himself 'The Greatest'?

4 Where would you see a short extra cover and a square leg?

5 In May 1985, from whom did Kenny Dalglish take over as manager of Liverpool Football Club?

6 In a standard pack of playing cards, if seventeen red cards have been played, how many red cards are left?

7 In showjumping, what is a 'puissance' event?

8 What is the fastest of all swimming strokes?

9 Which people gave us the sport of lacrosse? Was it the French, the Red Indians, or the Egyptians?

10 In which year did Duncan Goodhew win the Olympic swimming 'gold' for Britain?

11 Where were the summer Olympics of 1980 held?

12 In which sport have Clare Francis and Naomi James made their names?

GAME FOUR   POP MUSIC (2)

1   Who is Radio One's longest-serving D.J?

2   Julio Iglesias had a chart hit with a well-known country and western singer. Who was he?

3   What is the name of the fellow West Indian with whom Joan Armatrading formed a song-writing partnership early in her career?

4   With which female artist did Duran Duran tour in 1980?

5   To whom is Chrissie Hynde married?

6   Michael Jackson never eats meat. True or false?

7   Name Tom Petty's backing group.

8   What is the name of the part played by Madonna in the film *Who's that girl*?

9   Why was Madonna's husband Sean Penn in prison in August 1987?

10   In which country was Johnny Logan, twice winner of the Eurovision Song Contest, born?

11   For whom did Stevie Wonder sing 'Happy Birthday'?

12   What is the title of the debut album by Jesus and Mary Chain?

1   What causes adrenalin to be released by a gland in the body?

2   Whose interests are protected by the Geneva Conventions?

3   Not counting the Vatican, how many States share a border with Italy?

4   What is the first name of Barney Flintstone's wife?

5   In the alphabet, 'A' is to 'F' as which letter is to 'Z'?

6   What kind of schools is Robert Raikes credited with founding around two hundred years ago?

7   If you're facing north and turn right till you face north-west, through how many degrees of a circle do you turn?

8   Which Sign of the Zodiac comes between Virgo and Scorpio?

9   What was the first name of Prime Minister Disraeli?

10   Until the 1930s, it was called Persia. What do we call that country nowadays?

11   When Edward Heath was Prime Minister, which woman was Education Minister?

12   In proverbs, which number do you get if you add the number of birds in the bush to the stitches saved by one in time?

GAME FIVE

1   Who would apply to be Steward of the Manor of Northstead?

2   Which member of the Royal Family was married on 14 November 1973?

3   Which two nations did Napoleon defeat at the Battle of Austerlitz?

4   What is the second biggest city in Russia?

5   In which of the Houses of Parliament is the Queen's Speech made at the start of each Session?

6   In the saying, who do you rob to pay Paul?

7   In which kind of variety act would you expect to see Lord Charles?

8   In the traditional song, who was 'like a fairy, And her shoes were number nine'?

9   What relation is the Queen to the Duke of Kent?

10   If you placed a row of 50-pence pieces in a straight line, how many complete coins would fit into the length of a metre?

11   In the orchestra, what kind of instrument is a tam-tam?

12   On television's *Kids of Degrassi Street*, in which city is Degrassi Street?

GAME FIVE   POP MUSIC (1)

1 What milestone did Cliff Richard reach in August 1987 when he released 'Some people'?

2 Which Marillion album included the hit single 'Warm wet circles'?

3 Name Frankie Goes To Hollywood's lead singer.

4 What was the title of Duran Duran's number one single in April 1984?

5 What was Simple Minds' first chart entry?

6 What title has Aretha Franklin earned in the field of soul music?

7 Where was Joan Armatrading born?

8 What do the initials R.E.M., as used in the name of a well-known group, normally stand for?

9 Name R.E.M's songwriter.

10 Name the writer of Tina Turner's 1985 smash hit, 'What's love got to do with it?'

11 How many people with the surname 'Taylor' were in the group Duran Duran?

12 Which of Marvin Gaye's hits reached number eight in 1986?

GAME FIVE   NEWS OF THE '80s

1   What was awarded to Desmond Tutu in 1984, Mother Teresa of Calcutta in 1979 and Martin Luther King in 1964?

2   In Britain, who was elected leader of the Social Democratic Party in 1983?

3   In which year did he resign as leader?

4   The Prime Minister of a European country was murdered while walking home from a cinema in 1986. In which country did this happen?

5   In 1986, which girl rock star portrayed Annie Oakley in a British production of the musical *Annie Get Your Gun*?

6   Which musical work by Andrew Lloyd Webber had its world premiere at St Thomas's Church in New York In 1985?

7   Who was murdered by Mark Chapman in New York in February 1980?

8   Of which Commonwealth country did Robert Hawke become Prime Minister in 1983?

9   What big event took place at 11.30 am in London on 23 July 1986?

10   What is the first name of the Soviet leader, Mr Gorbachev?

11   In the Soviet Union in recent years, *glasnost* has been much in the news. What is *glasnost*?

12   Which new title did the Queen give Princess Anne in the summer of 1987?

GAME FIVE   MOVIES

1 Which film musical gave us the song 'Bless Your Beautiful Hide'?

2 In *The Sound of Music*, how many children were in the von Trapp family?

3 Who starred with Oliver Reed and John Tavolta in *Two of a Kind*?

4 Which fictitious hero was the subject of the 1984 film *Greystoke*?

5 Who played James Bond in *Never Say Never Again*?

√ 6 What do the initials BAFTA stand for in the world of the arts?

7 Which 1987 film told the story of rock'n'roll singer Ritchie Valens?

8 Who was the folk singer who starred in *Hearts of Fire*?

9 Complete the title of the Michael J Fox comedy that begins *The Secret of* ...

10 Anthony Perkins took the lead in 1983 in a follow up to which classic spine-tingling film?

11 In which film did Huey Lewis and the News sing 'The Power of Love'?

12 In the Disney film *Pinocchio* what kind of animal was J. Worthington Foulfellow?

GAME FIVE   SPORTS AND GAMES

1   If Alan Minter met Charlie Magri, which sport would you expect them to talk about?

2   Which major sporting event of 1986 was centred round the Meadowbank Stadium?

3   This century, which family have chased speed records in cars and boats called *Bluebird*?

4   What nationality is top tennis player Hana Mandlikova?

5   Add together the number of players in a rugby union side and a rugby league team, and what number should you get?

6   In which sport would you expect to see top competition at Henley in the first week of July each year?

7   What sport is the centre of attraction at Cowes Week?

8   In which sport is the international Davis Cup at stake?

9   Tessa Sanderson set an Olympic record in 1984 in which sport?

10   In which year did Jayne Torvill and Christopher Dean win both the World Ice-Dancing Championship and the Winter Olympics gold medal?

11   In October 1986, who retained the world chess championship?

12   Who set a world record of 357 wickets in cricket Test matches in the summer of 1986?

1 From where do Duran Duran take their name?

2 Out of which punk band did Simple Minds spring?

3 Name Frankie Goes To Hollywood's 1984 album.

4 Which number did Paul Hardcastle take to number one in 1985?

5 Simple Minds were the support act for which group during their 1984 US tour?

6 Name George Harrison's 1981 tribute single to John Lennon.

7 With which song did Jennifer Warnes and Joe Cocker have a chart hit in January 1983?

8 Of which group was Billy Idol a member before he went solo?

9 Three hit singles were released from the J. Geils Band's 1981 album 'Freeze Frame'. What were they?

10 Name the J. Geils Band vocalist who was sacked from the band in 1983 after sixteen years.

11 Where was Bryan Adams born?

12 Which famous female singer did Bryan Adams team up with for the hit 'It's only love'?

1   Which European nationality goes with beans, loaves and fries?

2   In which city is Britain's most northerly university?

3   Which organisation developed the Epcot Centre in America?

4   What is the name 'Epcot' short for?

5   How many masts would you expect to see on a ✓ sailing boat called a ketch?

6   Which part of the body sounds like an extra section at the end of a book?

7   Which religious reformer did the Lollards follow?

8   The French might call you a *poisson d'avril*. What would we call you in Britain?

9   Which four-letter word goes in front of soap, spot, drink and pedal?

10 What is unusual about the way the bird called the blue-footed booby keeps its eggs warm?

11 How many centimetres are in half a kilometre?

12 Who wrote the classic story of *The Water Babies*?

GAME SIX

1   Which boot is named after a Prime Minister?

2   On television, who has introduced the *Amazing Adventures of Morph*?

3   What kind of organisations were banned by the Combination Acts of 1799 and 1800?

4   Which Duke has his home at Woburn Abbey?

5   If mint sauce goes with lamb, which sauce usually goes with pork?

6   Which country of the United Kingdom has only six counties?

7   What item of clothing has been named after Bermuda?

8   In Roman numbers, which single letter do you get if you add LX to XL?

9   Which city gave the tangerine fruit its name?

10   To which European country do the Canary Islands belong?

11   How many books costing 99 pence each can I buy with £99.99?

12   In which city was the Archduke Francis Ferdinand assassinated, sparking off World War One?

GAME SIX   POP MUSIC (1)

1   Sheena Easton's 1980 hit '9 to 5' was re-titled for the US market. What was it called in America?

2   Simple Minds were one of the many groups that took part in Live Aid. Did they perform at Wembley or in Philadelphia?

3   Which D.J. refused to play Frankie Goes To Hollywood's first number one single?

4   'I heard it through the grapevine' was used to promote which article of clothing on TV?

5   Which war inspired '19' by Paul Hardcastle?

6   Name the two other ex-Beatles who guested on George Harrison's 'All those years ago'.

7   Jennifer Warnes was in the charts in November 1987 with a song called '(I've had) the time of my life'. With whom did she sing?

8   What was the title of the 1986 England World Cup Squad song?

9   David Essex had a hit in August 1983 called 'Tahiti'. From which West End musical show did it come?

10   In which year was 'I feel for you' a number one hit for Chaka Khan?

11   Who wrote Chaka Khan's hit 'I feel for you'?

12   Who performed the title song for the James Bond film *Living Daylights*?

1   How many games were played on the opening Monday of Wimbledon, 1987?

2   Who became Britain's Secretary of State for Energy in June 1987?

3   In which country did women stage a one-day strike in 1985 in protest at male privilege? Was it in Switzerland, Iceland or Denmark?

4   To which Cabinet post was Douglas Hurd appointed in 1985?

5   In which country was President Galtieri deposed in 1982?

6   Why did a visit by President Reagan to a European war cemetery cause controversy in May 1985?

7   Why was a £2 coin struck in Britain in 1986?

8   Which anniversary did the Girl Guides organisation celebrate in 1985?

9   In 1984, Dr David Jenkins was consecrated as Bishop of which city?

10 What kind of transport was the C5?

11 Which industrialist pioneered its development (though he's probably best known for work with calculators and computers)?

12 Which member of the Royal Family opened the new Falkland Islands airport in 1985?

1   Which comic actor starred as a headmaster in the 1986 film *Clockwise*?

2   In the title of Steven Spielberg's 1986 film, who was linked with the 'Pyramid of Fear'?

3   Which film won seven Oscars in 1986?

4   Which city was the setting for the musical *West Side Story*?

5   Which city completes the title of the Madonna movie – – – – – – – – *Surprise*?

6   Pop star Michael Jackson made his debut as a film ✓ actor in *The Wiz*. Of which film was it a remake?

7   In film comedy, who was the partner of the man born Arthur Stanley Jefferson?

8   Which cartoon star was born in a circus train and had ears so big he used them as wings?

9   In which Disney film do we meet O'Malley the alley cat?

10 In which country was film star Julie Christie born?

11 Which British city was the setting for the film *Letter to Brezhnev*?

12 In which series of films do we meet Miss Moneypenny and 'M'?

GAME SIX   SPORTS AND GAMES

1   In sport, what is the PGA?

2   In the Sport Aid cricket match of May 1986, David Gower captained the Rest of the World against which team?

3   In a game of dominoes, I hold all seven dominoes with a blank on them. What do the spots of all seven add up to?

4   Which boxing weight has the same name as a kind of poultry?

5   At the beginning of a game of draughts, how many squares of the board are empty?

6   In which game do competitors start at 301 and finish at 'zero'?

7   Which sport was described by Oscar Wilde as 'the unspeakable in pursuit of the uneatable'?

8   What is to badminton as a puck is to ice hockey?

9   Across the Atlantic, the Chicago Bears have reached the top in which sport?

10   In the 1984 Olympics, who won the men's 1500 metres for Britain?

11   In which year was football's World Cup competition last held?

12   In the final of that World Cup, who did Argentina beat?

GAME SIX   POP MUSIC (2)

1 Which 'Lord's' voice features on Paul Hardcastle's 'Just for the money'?

2 Name Bryan Adams' songwriting partner.

3 What is Prince's full name?

4 With which song did Billy Joel have a number one hit in October 1983?

5 Which member of Abba was involved in writing music for the West End musical *Chess*?

6 To what did the '19' of Paul Hardcastle's hit refer?

7 Name Bad Manners' vocalist.

8 From which country do A-Ha come?

9 What is the name of Michael Jackson's manager?

10 What was Chris de Burgh's number one hit in July 1986?

11 Name the member of the legendary Beach Boys who tragically drowned in California in December 1983.

12 Which band was Paul Young a member of immediately before he went solo?

GAME SIX   GENERAL KNOWLEDGE (2)

1   Which Continent is 'home' to the guinea-pig?

2   In stories, which of the 'Famous Five' has four legs?

3   By which name are Phyllis, Peter and Roberta known in the title of the book by E. Nesbit?

4   Which language gave us the word 'shampoo'? Was it Chinese, Hindi or Egyptian?

5   Only one of these four countries has the pound as its unit of money; the rest use the dollar. Which is the odd country out from Singapore, Sudan, New Zealand and Australia?

6   In Tom Paxton's song 'Daddy's taking us to the zoo tomorrow', what do you see all the monkeys doing?

7   When a butterfly is at rest, are its wings usually horizontal, vertical or at 45 degrees?

8   Which two continents are separated by the Bering Strait?

9   If Inverness has a cape and Guernsey has a jersey, what does Norfolk have?

10   Which English county has its council headquarters at Northallerton?

11   In the Bible, the Book of Jude is in the New Testament. True or false?

12   In Roman legend, whose wife was Juno?

GAME SEVEN

1 In many countries, this day is known as 'Mardi Gras'. What do we call it?

2 What was the name of the wife of Louis the Sixteenth of France, who died in 1793?

3 In which present-day country did the ancient Aztec race mainly live?

4 Which letter follows next in this series: O T T F . . .?

5 In the 1930s, in what field was Amy Johnson a pioneer?

6 The semi-precious stone of jade is usually in shades of which colour?

7 Which country was the birthplace of Mother Teresa, famous for her work with poor people in Calcutta?

8 Which capital city stands on the River Rhine and was the birthplace of Beethoven?

9 Where would you find a continental shelf?

10 How many King Georges have reigned in Britain this century?

11 What do the initials CBI stand for?

12 What were the first names of the two Wesley brothers who developed the Methodist religious movement?

GAME SEVEN   POP MUSIC (1)

1   Name Frankie Goes To Hollywood's producer.

2   What was Paul Hardcastle's chart follow-up to '19'?

3   What was Bryan Adams' first UK chart hit?

4   'I've had the time of my life', sung by Bill Medley and Jennifer Warnes, was the love theme to which movie?

5   With which famous country and western artist did Sheena Easton sing in 1983?

6   Which group perform over the closing credits of the James Bond film *Living Daylights*?

7   Madonna used to work in a food shop in Times Square, New York. What type of food did the shop sell?

8   Who married Renate Blauel in Sydney, Australia in 1984?

9   Where was Howard Jones born?

10   What was Howard Jones' job before he became a successful pop artist?

11   Aled Jones reached number five in the charts in November 1985 with which song?

12   What was the title of Prince's semi-autobiographical film?

GAME SEVEN   NEWS OF THE '80s

1   The 40th anniversary of V-E Day was celebrated in 1985. What do the letters VE stand for?

2   During the 1980s, which rather metallic–sounding nickname was given by the Russians to Mrs Thatcher?

3   Which big advertising campaign of 1986 asked us to 'tell Sid', if we saw him?

4   Who became British Shadow Foreign Secretary in July 1987?

5   Which book by Peter Wright was in the headlines in 1987?

6   In which year was Ronald Reagan first elected President of the USA?

7   In 1984, which Indian city was the scene of a gas-leak tragedy in which thousands died?

8   What was the name of the ship whose sinking during the Falklands conflict came under detailed scrutiny by Mr Tam Dalyell MP and others?

9   The much-loved comedy partner of Ernie Wise died in 1984. Who was he?

10   Which musical show opened in London in March 1984 and is still running – with the cast on roller skates?

11   Why was Geraldine Ferraro in the international spotlight in 1984?

12   A Frenchman called Stephane Peyron completed a solo pioneering crossing of the Atlantic in the summer of 1987. Did he travel by canoe, by sailboard or in a bath?

1 Which great film actor and comedian who died in 1987 was born David Daniel Kaminsky?

2 What kind of 'pursuits' formed the title of the film starring Tom Conti and Helen Mirren?

3 What was America's top box office film success of 1985?

4 Why did *The Jazz Singer* mark a cinema milestone in 1927?

5 Who directed the 1985 film *The Color Purple*?

6 In the film *Top Gun*, what kind of fighters were competing against each other?

7 Can you name the 1986 British musical based on teenagers' lives in the 1950s?

8 Which pop star played the villain in that musical?

9 Who took the part of the adventurous youngster who travelled Back to the Future in the film of that name?

10 Who wrote the original books on which the 1986 film *Biggles* was based?

11 What colour of cauldron featured in the title of a 1985 Disney film?

12 In which film did we meet a bear called Tenderheart, as well as Lotsa Heart Elephant?

GAME SEVEN   SPORTS AND GAMES

1   Which pop star's yacht crossed the finishing line third in May 1986 after the Whitbread round-the-world race?

2   What was the name of the pop star's yacht?

3   Which football team did Terry Venables take to the European Cup Final of 1986?

4   Who was Britain's Sportsman of the Year of 1985?

5   In 1983, Britain's Sportswoman of the Year was from the tennis world. Who was she?

6   Traditionally, what kind of sporting event do the Royal Family attend on the first Saturday of September each year?

7   In 1987, where was the Horse of the Year Show held in Britain?

8   Which world title did Joe Johnson win in May 1986?

9   In June 1986, who replaced David Gower as England's cricket captain?

10   Which of these sports stars is youngest: Ian Botham, Steve Cram or Steve Davis?

11   If a dice comes to rest with the 'four' on top, which number is hidden under the dice?

12   Whose life story was told by Dick Francis in a book called *Lester*?

1 Which college did Sheena Easton attend before becoming a pop star?

2 What did Billy Joel suffer while recording his 1982 album 'The Nylon Curtain'?

3 Prince was in the charts in September 1987 with a song called 'U got the look'. Who did he sing with on this record?

4 Name the two hit singles from the film *Purple Rain*.

5 What is Buster Bloodvessel's real name?

6 Name Chris de Burgh's Christmas hit of 1986.

7 Who masterminded the band Bow Wow Wow?

8 What was Bow Wow Wow's first single?

9 With whom did David Bowie have a Christmas hit in 1982, entitled 'Peace on earth'?

10 What was David Bowie doing with Mick Jagger at number one in the charts in September 1985?

11 Can you name the well-known guitarist who performs on Mike Post's *Hill Street Blues* TV theme?

12 In which US TV detective series did Phil Collins make a modest appearance?

1   In English, which boy's name corresponds to the Latin Jacobus?

2   What colour are the flowers of the laburnum?

3   In which country was the Battle of Flodden fought in 1513?

4   In which field did John Maynard Keynes, Lord Keynes, who died in 1946, make his name?

5   Which large wild animal's name means literally 'nose horn'?

6   In stories by Jill Murphy, what kind of witch was Mildred Hubble?

7   If Guy Fawkes Day is a Wednesday, on which day of the week does Christmas Eve fall the same year?

8   Four States of the USA have names beginning with 'New'. Can you name them?

9   Which musical instrument is Julian Bream best known for playing?

10   Which five-letter word can mean either a theatre seat, a place for an animal or a booth to sell goods?

11   Does a bryologist study mosses, babies or horses?

12   On which everyday objects will you find Latin words meaning 'ornament and safeguard'?

GAME EIGHT

1   Which country calls itself the Hellenic Republic?

2   What is the most abundant metal in the crust of the earth?

3   What would you expect to happen to the metal gallium if you held some in your hand?

4   What is a Brazilian howler? Is it a bad mistake in school in Rio de Janeiro, an owl or a monkey?

5   Does buttermilk contain butter?

6   In the song that begins 'I peeped in to say goodnight', what gift was the young girl hoping for?

7   Two of the United States of America begin with a 'K'. Which is first in alphabetical order?

8   How many of these four cities are capitals: Ottawa, Geneva, Kampala and Lusaka?

9   Which continent gave the English language the word 'zombie'?

10 If you wrote 'ten to the power of ten' full out in figures, how many noughts would you write?

11 In the alphabet, of which Roman emperor ought the letters 'N' and 'P' remind you?

12 How many leap years will there be between 1989 and 1999?

GAME EIGHT   POP MUSIC (1)

1 What was the name of the BBC programme that helped Sheena Easton to stardom?

2 Which organisation invited Wham to perform in Peking in 1985?

3 Name Howard Jones' debut album.

4 From which cartoon film did Aled Jones' hit 'Walking in the air' come?

5 Who wrote music to the horror movie *The Burning* in 1982?

6 From which country does Chris de Burgh come?

7 What was the title of Paul Young's first solo album?

8 Name the two artists that made up the group Yazoo.

9 Name XTC's only top ten hit to date.

10 Name Spandau Ballet's lead singer.

11 In which year did Spandau Ballet reach number one with 'True'?

12 Lionel Ritchie's hit 'Say you, say me' came from which film?

GAME EIGHT   NEWS OF THE '80s

1   The illness of AIDS has been in the news in recent years. What do the letters A I D S stand for?

2   How did Svetlana Savitskaya make history on 25 July, 1984?

3   What was the name of the Poet Laureate who died in May 1984?

4   In which county of Central America have Contra rebels opposed President Ortega?

5   Former Barnardo's boy Bruce Oldfield organised a big show of his work in 1985 to benefit the Barnardo's Homes. In which field has Bruce reached the top?

✓ 6   Who was the star of the show *Barnum* in London?

7   In 1981, President Sadat was assassinated while watching a military parade. Of which country was he president?

8   In 1980, India returned a woman Prime Minister to power. Who was she?

9   In which year did it become compulsory to wear front seat belts in cars?

10   Queen Beatrix became sovereign of which European country in 1980?

11   In 1987, on which island have the 'Tamil Tigers' been in the news as a rebel group?

12   How many Walton girls reached the world's headlines when they were born at Liverpool in November 1983?

GAME EIGHT   MOVIES

1   What is the connection between the stories of the James Bond films and *Chitty Chitty Bang Bang*?

2   Which hit stage musical did Richard Attenborough bring to the cinema screen in 1986?

3   Which girl's name completes the film title: *Desperately Seeking . . .*?

4   Which country is the setting for Richard Attenborough's 1987 film 'Cry freedom'?

5   In *The Goonies*, what did the children find that sent them on a treasure hunt?

6   Which 1985 film told the story of the composer Mozart?   ✓

7   What was the setting for Julian Mitchell's 1984 film *Another Country*?

8   In the 1984 film *Bounty*, who played Captain Bligh?

9   Which 1985 film was subtitled 'Electric Boogaloo'?

10   In 1985, George C Scott starred in a film version of a story by Dickens. What was its title?

11   How many earlier British film versions have been made of that story?

12   Which Coppola film of 1985 told of the career of jazz cornettist Dixie Dwyer?

GAME EIGHT   SPORTS AND GAMES

1 Which sport is the book known as *Wisden* about?

2 Football: in which playing position has Pat Jennings been an international star for Northern Ireland?

3 How old was Boris Becker when he won the Wimbledon men's singles in 1985?

4 Which game begins at the 20th letter of the alphabet?

5 A frisbee champion will aim to get a good MTA. What do these letters stand for?

6 In which sport have Steffi Graf and Gabriela Sabatini reached the top?

7 For which country has football international Charlie Nicholas played?

8 Which kind of shoe sounds like a sports coach?

9 Which English city lost its bid to host the 1992 Olympics?

10 Which European city will in fact be the scene of the 1992 summer Olympics?

11 In September of 1986, who became world welterweight boxing champion?

12 At the opening of the 1984 Winter Olympics, who was Britain's flag bearer?

GAME EIGHT   POP MUSIC (2)

1   Paul Young had a hit in 1985 with a song entitled 'Every time you go away'. Who wrote the song?

2   Who wanted to 'wake up with you' in July 1986?

3   Which rock singer took part in the Broadway production of *The Pirates of Penzance*?

4   She travelled on Jefferson Airplane and on Jefferson Starship, ending up on Starship. Who is she?

5   He started life as Declan MacManus, but by which name is he better known in the music business?

6   'Wired for sound' was a hit for whom in 1981?

7   In whose house was the musician Michael Rudetski found dead in August 1986?

8   How many top ten hits in both the UK and the USA did Michael Jackson have from his album 'Thriller'?

9   After what are the Thompson Twins named?

10   From where do the group New Model Army take their name?

11   Who was lead singer with Kajagoogoo?

12   Why was Bow Wow Wow's first single not really a single?

1   In which ocean does the island of Madagascar lie?

2   In geometry, how many faces does the solid figure called a tetrahedron have?

3   What is the usual name for the twelve teeth which are nearest the back of your mouth?

4   If a composer marks music *pianissimo*, how does he want it played?

5   In which television series was a baby called Vicki Louise born in May 1986?

6   On a boat with three masts, would you find the mizen mast nearest the bows, nearest the stern or in the middle?

7   What do Tin Lizzies have in common with Beetles?

8   If you see a car with the international registration letters IL, where does it come from?

9   Apart from 'dog watches', what's the usual length of a 'watch' in ship's time?

10   In which famous art gallery can you see the portrait of the Mona Lisa?

11   What is a 'mahout'?

12   In the traditional American song, from which State do I come with 'my banjo on my knee'?

GAME NINE

1   What can lie on its back, eight feet up in the air?

2   What are mudskippers? Are they fish, crabs or frogs?

3   In America, how many nickels are in a dollar?

4   Which BBC disc jockey has the same name as a huntsman of traditional song?

5   What makes bees buzz?   ✓

6   On television, which comedian has claimed his sketches are 'all in the best possible taste'?

7   If three sides of a square add up to 96 centimetres, how long is half of the fourth side?

8   How many humps has an Arabian camel?

9   In the 'Mr Men' stories by Roger Hargreaves, what does Mr Bump wear on his head?

10 Which letter of the alphabet sounds like a tree?

11 Two brothers' ages add up to twenty, and one is six years older than the other. What is the age of the younger brother?   ✓

12 In Roald Dahl's tale *Fantastic Mr Fox*, what is the occupation of Mr Boggis, Mr Bunce and Mr Bean?

1 For which James Bond film did Sheena Easton sing the title song?

2 What is the name of the girl vocalist with the group T'Pau?

3 Of what is 'Limahl' an anagram?

4 Name Paul Young's backing band.

5 In 1986, Jean Michel Jarre gave the biggest concert ever by a single artist. Where was it held?

6 Which two artists had a top ten hit with the theme from the film *Endless Love* in September 1981?

7 In which year was *The Face* first published?

8 Who is Martin Lee Aday?

9 In which group was Colin Hay the lead singer?

10 From which continent do Men at Work come?

11 Which continent were Toto singing about in February 1983?

12 Who had a hit with an elephant which packed its trunk in December 1984?

GAME NINE   NEWS OF THE '80s

1   In October 1983, who came first in a vote in which Mr Hattersley was second, Mr Heffer third and Mr Shore fourth?

2   What kind of camp was in the news at Greenham Common during the 1980s?

3   Which best-selling author became deputy chairman of the Conservative Party in 1985?

4   In 1984, why did Indian troops storm the Golden Temple in Amritsar?

5   During the 1980s, which British industry claimed: 'We're getting there!' in an advertising slogan?

6   Which member of the Royal Family rode to their first racing victory at Redcar in August 1986?

7   In 1986, which British nuclear reprocessing plant was closed after radioactivity was said to be above the safety limits?

8   In which year of the 1980s was Prince William born?

9   In the same year of Prince William's birth, whose flagship was raised from the seabed and taken into Portsmouth Harbour?

10 Which 'Warrior' was sunk at New Zealand in 1985?

11 Why did the President of France and Mrs Thatcher go together to the Chapter House of Canterbury Cathedral on 12 February 1986?

12 Which new tabloid colour newspaper was published in Britain for the first time in March 1986?

GAME NINE   MOVIES

1 Who directed the film comedy *Comfort and Joy*?

2 What kind of 'war' is at the centre of the *Comfort and Joy* plot?

3 In the 1984 Christmas box-office hit, how many 'Ghostbusters' were there?

4 Complete the title of this film of 1985: *Give My Regards to . . .*

5 Which pop star wrote the screenplay for that *Give My Regards to . . .* film?

6 Which Spielberg movie told of havoc in the town of Kingston Falls, caused by a Christmas present?

7 Name two of the three locations where the action of *Indiana Jones and the Temple of Doom* takes place.

8 Which David Puttnam film was based on a 1980 *New York Times* prize-winning article called 'The Death and Life of Dith Pran'?

9 The film *1984* – released in 1984 – was the last film of which great actor?

10 Who wrote the original novel on which *A Passage To India* was based?

11 Who directed the film *A Passage To India*?

12 Which 1985 film was all about the kidnapping of a pig?

GAME NINE   SPORTS AND GAMES

1   After which kind of antelope are South African sportspeople sometimes nicknamed?

2   In 1982, David Moorcroft took just .41 of a second more than 13 minutes to set a world record in Oslo. What was the race?

3   Who won the 1984 men's singles final at Wimbledon?

4   On which day of the week is the University Boat Race traditionally held?

5   Why was the race postponed for a day in 1984?

6   What do the letters BMX stand for?

7   What is the usual name for the track in downhill skiing?

8   Which American sport is sometimes known as Gridirons?

9   In June 1985, which British boxer won the world featherweight title?

10   In which sport has Alain Prost held a world title?

11   In 1985, which British athlete broke three world records in less than three weeks?

12   What is the only chess piece which can jump over other pieces?

GAME NINE   POP MUSIC (2)

1 Marvin Gaye's 1982 hit 'Sexual healing' won which Grammy award?

2 Who sang the theme song to the movie *Fame*?

3 Who were 'Walking the dinosaur' in October 1987?

4 Who guested with Clannad on their 1985 hit 'In a lifetime'?

5 Name the two members of the group Erasure.

6 What was the title of the Jacksons' 1984 US tour?

7 Paul Simon's 1986 album was named Graceland, after a famous rock star's house. Who lived in this house?

8 What is the title of Bob Geldof's autobiography?

9 Who sings the theme music to the TV series *Moonlighting*?

10 Who wrote the original theme music to Terry Wogan's BBC TV show?

11 Which Chinese-sounding band had a hit with 'Dance hall days' in 1984?

12 What do the initials E.L.O. stand for?

GAME NINE   GENERAL KNOWLEDGE (2)

1   Why do emus never fly over water?

2   The names of three States of the USA end in the letter 'i'. Name two of them.

3   In the TV series *'Allo, 'Allo*, what were the first names of the original two waitresses in Rene's cafe?

4   Which State of Australia was once called Van Diemen's Land?

5   With a disc film newly in your camera, how many pictures could you take?

6   Which television comedy series is about Beryl and Arthur Crabtree's family?

7   Which of these cities lies furthest west – Vienna, Copenhagen or Berlin?

8   In Shakespeare's *Hamlet*, which words complete the line 'To be or not to be'?

9   In television's *Cagney and Lacey*, what is the first name of Sergeant Cagney?

10   According to the carol, of all the trees that are in the wood, which bears the crown?

11   Which British composer wrote *The Dream of Gerontius*?

12   Which five-letter word that describes a shape can also mean a set of drinks and part of a boxing contest?

GAME TEN

✓

1   Which song mentions a jumbuck in a tucker-bag?

2   How many major planets revolve round the Sun?

3   Which King Henry of England won the Battle of Agincourt?

4   In the European Economic Community, what do the initials CAP stand for?

✓5   In which mountainous region do the Basque people live?

6   In 1988, how old is Noddy – 39, 49 or 59?

7   Which instrument will a doctor probably use if he examines you by auscultation?

8   Who is the second in line to the throne?

9   Which famous 'Express' ran between Sacramento in California and St Joseph, Missouri, in the early 1860s?

10   Which well-known fable about two creatures illustrates the proverb 'Slow and steady wins the race'?

11   For which political party is Cyril Smith a Member of Parliament?

12   Which popular breakfast food shares its name with a formal drink?

GAME TEN   POP MUSIC (1)

1 Who teamed up with Freddie Mercury in the autumn of 1987 to sing about 'Barcelona'?

2 In the title of an album released in 1986, what did Elvis Costello crown himself?

3 Name Bob Seger's backing band.

4 What is the name of the stylist/artist who masterminded Grace Jones and her image?

5 What is the name of Paul Young's keyboard player and co-writer?

6 David Bowie's hit 'Underground' came from which film?

7 Name the composer of the 1986 number one 'The Chicken Song'.

8 What was the title of *Miami Vice* star Don Johnson's 1986 album?

9 Which Eurythmics album included their hit 'Here comes the rain again'?

10 Who is Talking Heads' lead guitarist and vocalist?

11 Young Steve and the Afternoon Boys had a minor hit in 1982 with 'I'm alright'. Who is 'Young Steve'?

12 On which album was Peter Gabriel's hit 'Sledgehammer'?

GAME TEN   NEWS OF THE '80s

1　How did an international incident grow out of a South Korean jumbo jet flight in September 1983?

2　Jacqueline du Pré, who died in 1987, was world famous for her skill at playing which musical instrument?

3　In 1984, lightning was blamed for a fire which badly damaged a famous British church. Which church?

4　Whose painting *Irises* was sold for over £30 million in 1987?

5　Where did a bedroom discussion take place in 1982 which led to public concern about the safety of the Royal Family?

6　Since the beginning of 1980, how many leaders has the Labour Party had in Britain?

7　In the summer of 1986, a major sporting event in Britain was boycotted by several overseas countries. What was the event?

8　Which of the Queen's children celebrated a 21st birthday in 1985?

9　In 1985, which British star's show won the major television prize known at the 'Golden Rose of Montreux'?

10　In 1983, of which country did Menachem Begin resign as Prime Minister?

11　What happened to the Greater London Council on 1 April 1986?

12　In a 1986 portrait of the Queen, she was accompanied by Spark. Who or what was Spark?

GAME TEN   MOVIES

1   In the 1987 comedy-adventure film *Ishtar*, what was the occupation of the two characters played by Dustin Hoffman and Warren Beatty?

2   In the 1984 film *Reuben, Reuben*, who played a drunken Scots poet?

3   What is the middle name of top director Francis Coppola?

4   In the film *A Private Function*, what was the profession of Michael Palin?

5   In which South American country was much of the action of *Romancing the Stone* set?

6   Which 'Party' on film in 1985 starred James Mason, John Gielgud and Edward Fox?

7   What was unusual about the heroine in *Splash*? ✓

8   Which *Star Trek* film was sub-titled 'The Search for Spock'?

9   Which film had *Indiana Jones and the Temple of Doom* as its sequel?

10   In which 'super' role did Helen Slater star in 1984?

11   What was the 1985 sequel to *2001: A Space Odyssey*?

12   Who wrote the songs for *The Woman in Red* in 1984?

GAME TEN   SPORTS AND GAMES

1   Over which course is the classic horse race of the Derby run?

2   In which sport would you come across a 'popping crease'?

3   Who rode a horse called Priceless to the world three-day event title in 1986?

4   In the game of Monopoly, what are the two 'utilities'?

5   In which sport has Beryl Crockford crossed the winning line backwards many times?

6   Who were the finalists in cricket's World Cup of 1987?

7   Add the two scores which make 'deuce' in tennis, and what number do you get?

8   If you decide to go on a 'yomp', should you get a saddle, a pair of stout walking boots or a life-jacket?

9   Which place name links Bulgaria with Tobermory and Navratilova?

10   For which nation was Diego Maradona a star in the football World Cup of 1986?

11   Which number do you get if you add up the divisions in the English and Scottish senior football leagues?

12   Which tennis star was quoted as saying: 'My greatest strength is that I have no weaknesses'? Was it Jimmy Connors, Ivan Lendl, or John McEnroe?

GAME TEN   POP MUSIC (2)

1   What was the title of David Byrne's first feature film?

2   Name all the members of the band Brown Sauce who had a hit with 'I wanna be a winner'.

3   Berlin's hit 'Take my breath away' came from which film?

4   Name the three members of Genesis.

5   Which Dire Straits' album contains their number two hit 'Walk of Life'?

6   Name the Beastie Boys' first LP.

7   Who is the female singer of the Cocteau Twins?

8   Who had a hit with 'Brother Louie' in 1986?

9   Name the US heavy metal band with a strong religious bias.

10   Which famous jazz saxophonist played the music from the film *Round Midnight*?

11   What is Quincy Jones' nickname for Michael Jackson?

12   What is the title of Bob Geldof's 1986 solo album?

1. Of which vegetable is broccoli a hardy variety?

2. One of Britain's biggest companies is ICI. What do the initials stand for?

3. Is a porcupine a rodent?

4. If a stereo unit costing £250 has its price increased by eight per cent, how much will it cost?

5. Which Bohemian dance gave its name to a pattern of dots?

6. In the Bible, which is the first book of the Old Testament to have a man's name in its title?

7. What do we call the European capital the local people know as 'Wien'?

8. When King William the Fourth died, who came to the British throne?

9. In the sixteenth century, which South American Indian empire was conquered by Francisco Pizarro?

10. In the first six months of each year, how many months have 31 days?

11. Where was French revolutionary Jean Marat when Charlotte Corday murdered him? Was he in the bath, in church or at a ball?

12. Which item of clothing took its name from the Italian city of Genoa?

GAME ELEVEN

1   In cooking, which popular sauce is made from egg yolks, salad oil, vinegar or lemon juice and seasoning?

2   In which classic adventure book do we meet old Ben Gunn?

3   Which State of the USA shares a border with Arizona, Nevada and Oregon?

4   Which popular pet is also known as the 'jird' and the 'sand rat'?

5   In the Hans Andersen story, which little girl was found inside the petals of a flower?

6   Which word describing the pieces of a horse's harness can also mean a kind of nail?

7   According to Ogden Nash, which African animal is 'a homely beast – For human eyes he's not a feast'?

8   As a decimal, what is one per cent of one per cent of one per cent?

9   Which footwear sounds like an Irish accent?

10   Which Berkshire village gave its name to the Royal Military Academy?

11   In K M Peyton's book of the same name, what kind of creature is 'Fly-by-Night'?

12   What is the first name of the schoolboy who turns into Bananaman?

GAME ELEVEN   POP MUSIC (1)

1 What is the name of Elvis Costello's backing band?

2 Who had a Christmas hit with 'A winter's tale' in 1986?

3 Who did the Beach Boys team up with for their 1987 hit 'Wipeout'?

4 Which town do the Housemartins come from?

5 Style Council has two permanent members. Name them.

6 Name the member of Status Quo who left the band in 1982.

7 Which group evolved out of the Frantic Elevators?

8 Who had a hit with a green duck in December 1982?

9 What is Shakin' Stevens' real name?

10 Jennifer Rush and Huey Lewis and the News had a hit with different songs that had the same title. What was that title?

11 According to the title of their November 1985 chart hit, what were Jaki Graham and David Grant?

12 David Grant was originally in which group?

GAME ELEVEN   NEWS OF THE '80s

1   In 1986, the youngsters of television's *Grange Hill* recorded a song called 'Just Say No'. What message was the song trying to put across?

2   In which country did a heatwave in the summer of 1983 kill over 180 people?

3   What was the *White Crusader*, which carried Britain's colours in a major sporting contest of 1986?

4   Which *Discovery* left London in 1986 for a new home at Dundee?

5   What was the name of the event throughout 1985 which was known by the initials IYY?

6   According to the safety campaign of the 1980s, which single word should children say to strangers who ask youngsters to go with them?

7   In 1985, which University decided not to give an honorary doctorate to Mrs Thatcher?

8   In April 1984, which top British comedian – whose headgear was his trademark – died after collapsing on stage?

9   Who became engaged to Miss Diane Burgdorf in 1986?

10 During a visit to a European country in 1986, what did Mr Kinnock describe as 'stupidity turned into concrete'?

11 Which well-known pupil started at Wetherby School in London on 15 January 1987?

12 Still in 1987, which Hollywood superstar announced that she was to launch her own brand of perfume – and denied plans for a seventh marriage?

GAME ELEVEN   MOVIES

1   According to the title of the 1985 film who 'Just want to have fun'?

2   Was *Mad Max: Beyond Thunderdome* the second, third or fourth 'Max' film?

3   What nationality was the character played by Meryl Streep in *Out of Africa*?

4   Who starred as a romantic hunter in *Out of Africa*?

5   Which children's favourites are missing from the title of this 1986 film: *The – – – – – – – Take Manhattan*?

6   In which country was the 1985 comedy *Restless Natives* set?

7   What transport was used by the 'highwaymen' in *Restless Natives*?

8   Who plays Kirk in the *Star Trek* films?

9   What were the first names of the two children in *Mary Poppins*?

10   What was the first name of 'Crocodile' Dundee in the film of the same name?

11   Which dancer starred along with Debbie Reynolds and Donald O'Connor in the classic musical *Singing in the Rain*?

12   Which American singer and comedienne starred in the 1987 film *Outrageous Fortune* along with Shelley Long?

GAME ELEVEN   SPORTS AND GAMES

1 If you ran three marathons, how far to the *nearest* mile would you have travelled?

2 Which day of the week is part of the name of a Sheffield football club whose ground is at Hillsborough?

3 In which sport was Jackie Stewart a world champion before he retired in 1973?

4 Izaak Walton, who died in 1683, has been called 'the Father of . . .' which sport?

5 Who were the English football league champions of 1984/5?

6 Which world championship is played at the Crucible Theatre in Sheffield?

7 In golf, who is the 'Golden Bear'?

8 In March 1986, which British footballer joined Barcelona in a reported £2 million transfer?

9 Which 'Tip' won the Grand National of 1986?

10 Which 15-year-old British schoolgirl won a silver medal in the 1984 Olympics, and in which sport did she compete?

11 What is the nationality of racing driver Niki Lauda?

12 Three of Britain's national football teams took part in the 1986 World Cup finals. Which was the only British side to be missing?

GAME ELEVEN   POP MUSIC (2)

1   A Greek singer reached number two in the charts in January 1986 with 'Only Love'. Name her.

2   Which member of Wham had cosmetic surgery in 1984?

3   Which group was Paul Weller in before he formed Style Council?

4   Which instrument did John Coghlan play when he was a member of Status Quo?

5   For which major act were Pepsi and Shirley backing singers?

6   With which band did Feargal Sharkey once sing?

7   Which group was formed when Feargal Sharkey and Vince Clarke joined forces?

8   Who did Vangelis team up with in 1980?

9   Name Midge Ure's solo album of 1985.

10   Which singer left Van Halen in 1986?

11   On which 1983 hit did Eddie Van Halen join Michael Jackson?

12   Name the group that had a hit with 'Two pints of lager and a packet of crisps please'?

1   What does *Le Figaro* in France have in common with *Die Welt* in Germany and *La Stampa* in Italy?

2   If you put Snow White and her seven dwarfs in alphabetical order, who is last?   ✓

3   How many times higher than Snowdon is Mont Blanc – just over three times, four times or five times higher?

4   How many of King Henry the Eighth's children became monarchs of England?

5   In literature, what did Chekhov's 'Vanya' have in common with Joel Harris's 'Remus' and Harriet Beecher Stowe's 'Tom'?

6   In everyday language, what do we normally call the temperature at which liquid changes to solid?

7   What would an 'antitussive' medicine stop you doing?

8   If your parents had a silver wedding and your grand-parents a diamond wedding on the same day, for how many years in total would the couples have been married?

9   Whose catch-phrase is 'Fan-dabi-dozi'?

10   Which European capital is known as the 'Eternal City'?   ✓

11   If William Shakespeare had been born today, of which modern English county would he be a native?

12   In which century did the Grimm brothers produce their famous collection of fairy tales?

GAME TWELVE

1 On which everyday objects would you expect to see 'E' numbers?

2 Which Yorkshire town has the same name as the capital of the Canadian province of Nova Scotia?

3 What was the nickname of Ethelred, king of England from 978 till 1016 AD?

4 In which of the arts was Rodin famous?

5 Which measurement is .3048 of a metre?

6 Which African country lies across the Strait of Gibraltar from Europe?

7 In which modern country is the town of Tarsus, were St Paul was born?

8 How many days are there between Christmas Day and the following Valentine's Day?

9 In the satirical letters by Richard Ingrams and John Wells, who wrote to 'Dear Bill'?

10 If you buy a Mills and Boon book, what kind of story are you likely to find?

11 Which is bigger – a two-acre field, or a field of four hectares?

12 What do you get if you multiply the number of months of the year with an 'R' in their name by the number that don't have an 'R'?

GAME TWELVE   POP MUSIC (1)

1   Who wanted to 'free Nelson Mandela' in 1984?

2   Which band did the Beastie Boys tour with in 1987?

3   In 1987, Mel and Kim released an album entitled 'F.L.M.'. What do these initials stand for?

4   Name The Cure's lead singer.

5   In 1982, who said 'John Wayne is big leggy'?

6   In 1987, who sang 'Diamond lights'?

7   What is the relationship between the two members of The Proclaimers?

8   Give the surnames of reggae artists Sly and Robbie.

9   Name George Harrison's hit single of autumn 1987.

10 On the cover of the Pet Shop Boys' single 'Rent', on what are they standing?

11 Name the rock group that started the Live Aid concert from Wembley.

12 In 1985, George Michael won a song-writing award. What was it?

1 Why was journalist Nicholas Daniloff in the news in 1986?

2 Still in 1986, who was reported as saying: 'Why shouldn't men's underwear be fun'? Was it Kenny Everett, Esther Rantzen or the Princess of Wales?

3 In 1984, who did John Turner succeed as Prime Minister of Canada?

4 Which British writer won the Nobel Prize for Literature in 1983?

5 Which new national newspaper made its first appearance in Britain on 7 October 1986?

6 British driver Richard Noble set a new world land speed record in Nevada in October 1983. Was his new record 433, 533 or 633 miles per hour?

7 In 1986, who was quoted as saying: 'Margaret Thatcher is all right. I was going to live next door to her, but the garden was too small'. Was it: Simon Le Bon, Samantha Fox or Jimmy Savile?

8 Who resigned as Home Secretary in January 1986?

9 In January 1987, which industry agreed to cut back its sponsorship of sport?

10 Why did the then Health Secretary, Mr Norman Fowler, go to San Francisco early in 1987?

11 Late in 1985, who married Peter Holm?

12 President Botha of South Africa has been much in the news during the 1980s. By which two initials is he generally known?

GAME TWELVE   MOVIES

1   Which war was the backdrop for Marlon Brando's 1979 film *Apocalypse Now*?

2   What was the surname of pioneering film comedy brothers Chico, Harpo and Groucho?

3   On cinema screens in 1985, which film told about the enchanted world of a ten-year-old discovered in the pages of an old book?

4   In *Crocodile Dundee*, to which American city did reporter Sue Carlton take the Australian crocodile hunter?

5   In the 1982 Spielberg film who wanted to 'phone home'?

6   Which top Hollywood star became the real-life mayor of the town of Carmel?

7   Which director, who died in 1980, became famous for films like *Psycho* and *Rear Window*?

8   In which Disney film do we meet two dogs called Pongo and Perdita?

9   Who portrayed Indiana Jones in *Raiders of the Lost Ark*?

10   Who directed the Indiana Jones films?

11   Which well-known actress starred opposite Jack Nicholson in *Heartburn*?

12   In the film of *The Railway Children*, how many youngsters are in the family?

GAME TWELVE SPORTS AND GAMES

1 Which activity can you do with motorbikes that you can also do with eggs?

2 Who won the Open Golf Championship in Britain in 1984?

3 Which game is played on a diamond?

4 In 1987, which of these events was held last: the FA Cup Final, the Oaks or the British Grand Prix?

5 Which British ice skater was the men's Olympic champion of 1980?

6 What nationality is tennis star Ivan Lendl?

7 Of which British football club did Graeme Souness become player-manager in April 1986?

8 Which football club in England plays in the Scottish League?

9 At which boxing weight does Frank Bruno fight?

10 In which sport was Tracy Austin a young star of the late 1970s and early 1980s?

11 In which sporting event have Bill Beaumont and Emlyn Hughes been opposing captains in recent years?

12 Before Boris Becker, who was the last European to win the men's tennis singles at Wimbledon?

GAME TWELVE   POP MUSIC (2)

1 From which album does 'Sweetest smile', by Black, come?

2 What is the family name of Five Star?

3 What makes Gary Numan a high flyer?

4 What was Mel and Kim's disco hit of summer 1987?

5 What does the great BB King call his guitar?

6 What does the name Scritti Politti mean?

7 Which group was Jody Watley in before going solo?

8 What is Sting's real name?

9 Which band did Marc Almond team up with in 1985 to have the hit entitled 'I feel love'?

10 How high in the charts did 'Bette Davis eyes' by Kim Carnes reach?

11 With whom did Cherrelle sing 'Saturday love' in 1985?

12 Which Richard Rodgers tune is heard at the opening of the Dire Straits hit 'Tunnel of love'?

GAME TWELVE GENERAL KNOWLEDGE (2)

1 What nationality was the composer Borodin?

2 Which pair of creatures 'sailed away for a year and a day, To the land where the Bong-Tree grows'?

3 How many per cent is five per cent of twenty per cent?

4 Who was the last President of the United States from the Democratic Party?

5 In the Beaufort Scale of wind strength, which force represents a gale – is it Force Six, Eight or Twelve?

6 Which popular pet bird takes its name from the native Australian for 'good cockatoo'?

7 The French call it 'La Manche'. What is our name for it?

8 Which nursery rhyme character was alarmed by an arachnid of the order *Araneida*?

9 Were dinosaurs mammals?

10 Which two European countries are separated by a stretch of water called the Skagerrak?

11 How many people normally take part in an osculation?

12 Which creature moves more slowly – the two-toed sloth, or the three-toed sloth?

GAME THIRTEEN

1 In the titles of books by Mary Norton, who were Afield, Afloat, Aloft and Avenged?

2 At Saint Tiggywinkle's Hospital at Aylesbury, would you expect the patients to be dolls, hedgehogs or ducks?

3 If a farmer speaks about his 'Landrace gilt', what is he discussing?

4 What would you measure with an 'ombrometer' – darkness, rainfall or the strength of the wind?

5 In which year was *Top of the Pops* first broadcast on British television? Was it in 1954, 1964 or 1974?

6 Which of the Bronte sisters wrote the story *Wuthering Heights*?

7 Which word for a type of nobleman can also be a verb meaning 'to look closely'?

8 What are the two main vitamins to be found in cod liver oil?

9 Where in London is the Stone of Destiny?

10 Who is the famous husband of singer Sarah Brightman?

11 Which brass musical instrument sounds like an ice-cream?

12 If a clock strikes the number of each hour and once on each half-hour, how many times will it strike between five minutes after midnight and five past four in the morning?

GAME THIRTEEN   POP MUSIC (1)

1   Of which group was Randy Crawford a member before going solo?

2   Name Joan Jett's backing group.

3   Name Dead or Alive's debut album.

4   In 1985 Nick Kershaw sang about Sancho Panza's companion. Who was that companion?

5   What was Carole King before she became a recording artist?

6   What instrument does Mark King play?

7   On whose life was the film *A coal miner's daughter* based?

8   From where do Marillion take their name?

9   What was the best-selling pop single in the UK prior to 1984?

10   In 1987 Ozzy Osbourne released an album called 'Tribute'. Who was it a tribute to?

11   How many Pointer Sisters are there?

12   Who had a 'Hole in his shoe' in August 1984?

1   Why was Jambo from Jersey in the news in summer of 1986?

2   In 1984, who became the new Poet Laureate?

3   In which year was our last-but-one general election held?

4   In 1986, who became the first foreign king to address the British Parliament?

5   Which member of the Royal Family travelled in *Brazen Hussy*?

6   The African nation of Zimbabwe achieved independence in 1980. By which name was it known earlier?

7   In the early years of the 1980s, what was founded by the 'Gang of Four' in British politics?

8   In 1982, on which British river did a barrier against flooding come into operation at a cost of over £400 million?

9   From which State did President Marcos flee in February of 1986?

10   In 1987, on which occasion was the Princess of Wales quoted as saying: 'I'm as thick as a plank'?

11   The Duchess of Windsor, formerly Mrs Wallis Simpson, died in 1986 at her home in which capital city?

12   In 1987, where could you have bought an autumn crocus for 34 pence, and a North American blanket flower for 18 pence?

GAME THIRTEEN   MOVIES

✓ 1   Which charater did Dave Prowse play in *Star Wars*?

2   Who received a 'Best Actress' British Academy award for her part in the film *Educating Rita*?

3   Who starred with Ted Wass in the 1984 film of *The Curse of the Pink Panther*?

4   In the title of the film, what do the letters 'E.T.' stand for?

5   Which Superman film is sub-titled 'The Quest for Peace'?

6   In the films of the same name, who plays Rocky? ✓

7   In the 1987 film *Business as Usual*, in which kind of business does the story unfold?

8   In which 1983 film did John Travolta play the same role he took in *Saturday Night Fever*?

9   Which word is missing from the title of this 1987 Bob Dylan film: – – – – – – *of Fire*?

10   In which year was *The Sound of Music* released: was it 1955, 1960 or 1965?

11   In the films about him, what is the surname of that Beverly Hills Cop?

12   Who directed the 1987 Vietnam War drama *Full Metal Jacket*?

GAME THIRTEEN   SPORTS AND GAMES

1   Which city is next after Montreal, Moscow and Los Angeles?

2   Which nation won football's World Cup in 1982?

3   What was the name of the Aga Khan's top racehorse which went missing in Ireland in 1983?

4   In which sport might you have bogeys, birdies and dormies?

5   Which tennis star has been nicknamed 'Jimbo'?

6   In which sport did teenager Stephen Hendry become a star in the late 1980s?

7   Which game is said to have been invented by James Gibb, using cigar box tops and champagne corks on a dining table?

8   In sport, what has Rufus T. Firefly in common with Ernie Bilko and Arfur Daley?

9   Which sport won Olympic recognition in 1964 and has a name meaning literally 'the easy (or gentle) way'?

10 In poetry, which sport was Sir Henry Newbolt writing about in lines beginning: 'There's a breathless hush in the Close tonight'?

11 From which sport does the phrase 'to win hands down' come?

12 And which recreation gave us the phrase 'above board'?

GAME THIRTEEN   POP MUSIC (2)

1   What is Neil's real name?

2   Who are the members of Black Lace?

3   What was the Bluebell's one and only hit?

4   Who is the leader of Whitesnake?

5   Who produced the 1982 Dionne Warwick album 'Heartbreaker'?

6   What is the name of Mari Wilson's backing band?

7   Who wrote Robert Wyatt's minor hit of 1983?

8   Name the female singer with the band Monsoon, who had a 1982 hit with 'Ever so lonely'?

9   Name the founder and editor of the American rock magazine *Rolling Stone*.

10 From which country did Nena come?

11 What was the title of Heaven 17's debut album?

12 Which band was Charles Hodgson in before he formed Chas and Dave?

1   How many stars make up the constellation of the Plough?

2   What is the name of the ranch that's home to the Ewings in the TV soap opera *Dallas*?

3   Into which ocean does the River Zambezi flow?

4   Which colour would you expect a West Highland terrier to be?

5   What style of popular music has made singer Kenny Rogers well-known?

6   How many of King Henry the Eighth's wives were called Catherine?

7   The hunting leopard is said to be the fastest land mammal. By which name is it usually known?

8   What did Dr Edward Hunter invent that was called Hunter's Bend?

9   In which town was the school that originally inspired Ronald Searle to create St Trinian's? Was it in Bournemouth, Chester or Edinburgh?

10   What is the first name of Princess Margaret's daughter?

11   If you add the number of centimetres in a metre to the number of millimetres in a centimetre, which number should you get?

12   What is the lowest number of coins in general use which you need to pay a bill of 98 pence exactly?

GAME FOURTEEN

1 How many of these countries have a coastline: Czechoslovakia, Switzerland, Austria and Hungary?

2 In the 24-hour clock, how many minutes are there between 1020 hours and 2010 hours?

3 Which single word can mean a sausage, a firework or an old car?

4 What is the first name of President Reagan's wife?

5 What is measured by the Richter scale?

6 The French flag has red, white and blue stripes. Which one is in the middle?

7 In France, it's called the 'red fish', but what is our name for it?

8 Which Chinese official sounds like a kind of orange?

9 Which is the odd one out, Shetland, Exmoor, Connemara and Jersey?

10 How often does its value appear on a 20-pence coin?

11 Who wrote London's long-running play *The Mousetrap*?

12 Which part of a cacao tree gives us chocolate – the bark, the seeds or the root?

GAME FOURTEEN   POP MUSIC (1)

1   Who had a hit with 'O Superman' in 1981?

2   Who were the members of the duo Blancmange?

3   In what way is Rick Springfield well known in the US besides his career as a rock star?

4   With whom did Gary Moore have a 1985 hit called 'Out in the fields'?

5   Which group sang 'Eye of the tiger', the theme from the film *Rocky 3*?

6   Which group did a 'Farewell Tour' of the USA in 1982?

7   What is the middle name of Toyah Wilcox?

8   From where do Tears for Fears get their name?

9   What was the name of the TV pop show presented by Jools Holland?

10   What was the title of Blondie's last number one?

11   What was the title of Big Audio Dynamite's first hit?

12   What are the Christian names of Stock, Aitken and Waterman?

1 Which bank's shares went on sale to the public for the first time in 1986?

2 Which European border reopened in February of 1985 after 16 years?

3 In 1987, with which other British airline did British Airways want to merge?

4 Why did 6,000 children carry daffodils to Buckingham Palace in April 1986?

5 People known as 'yuppies' have been in the news in recent years: for which words is 'yuppies' an abbreviation?

6 Which national beauty queen won the Miss World title in 1987?

7 In January of 1986, which famous British ship found itself in an unusual role, helping people to safety during a civil war in South Yemen?

8 In which year of the 1980s did the national miners' strike begin in Britain?

9 Who was the chairman of the National Coal Board (now British Coal) at that time?

10 In November 1985, where did President Reagan meet Mr Gorbachev for the first East-West summit for over six years?

11 In 1986 George Younger succeeded Michael Heseltine in which Cabinet post?

12 Which member of the Royal Family took part in the radio programme *The Archers* in 1984?

GAME FOURTEEN   MOVIES

1   In which Muppet movie does Miss Piggy become a receptionist at a London fashion house run by Diana Rigg?

2   In the title of the 1987 film, which kind of 'Dancing' starred Jennifer Grey and Jerry Orbach?

3   In which movie did Sir John Mills star with Madonna?

4   In the 1980 film, at which sport did 'Gregory's Girl' excel?

5   Whose *Big Adventure* makes the title of a 1987 film starring Paul Rubens?

6   In which film did Katherine Hepburn win an Oscar for 'best actress' in 1981?

7   In *Top Gun*, who plays the daredevil leading character, 'Maverick' Mitchell?

8   As which Indian leader did Ben Kingsley star in a 1982 film?

9   In which movie did Timothy Dalton make his debut as James Bond?

10   In which film did the original 007 of the cinema, Sean Connery, star as a Franciscan monk mixed up in a murder mystery?

11   In the title of part five of the Star Wars film series, what does 'the empire' do?

12   Which 1987 film told a story of Britain during World War Two, as seen by a nine-year-old boy?

1   In the saying, which game goes with beer to symbolise an easy life?

2   Three distinct types of weapon are used in fencing. Two are the foil and the épée. What is the third?

3   Which sport is discussed in Act One of Shakespeare's *Henry the Fifth*? Is it boxing, golf or tennis?

4   What was the word coined by Stephen Potter to describe 'The Art of Winning Games Without Actually Cheating'?

5   On a standard darts board, what number do you get if you add the numbers on either side of 20?

6   Who was the last British player to win the women's tennis singles at Wimbledon?

7   Which sport would you expect to see at a velodrome?

8   If the Durham Wasps met the Dundee Rockets, what would the sport be?

9   Over which British golf course did Sandy Lyle win the Open of 1985?

10   In boxing, which weight is between bantamweight and lightweight?

11   In the 1986 football World Cup, who were runners-up?

12   In sport in Britain, what do the 'three As' stand for?

1 Name the dual writing/performing talents that formed the nucleus of Steely Dan.

2 From which Chris Rea album does 'Stainsby girls' come?

3 What is Mick Jagger's middle name?

4 With whom did Kim Wilde take 'another step closer'?

5 Who couldn't 'be with you tonight' in April 1987?

6 Who 'stripped' in March 1987?

7 Name the members of the group Wax.

8 With which band is Stevie Nicks mostly associated?

9 Name Status Quo's chart hit of December 1986.

10 Paul Medford and Letitia Dean had a hit in the charts in November 1986. Where do they more regularly appear?

11 Who was 'Pretty in pink' in September 1986?

12 On the cover of the Pet Shop Boys album 'Actually', what is Neil Tennant doing?

1   What is the first month of the year that has 30 days in it?

2   What is the popular name for the bone called the clavicle?

3   Who wrote the music for the show *Joseph and the Amazing Technicolour Dreamcoat*?

4   Which twentieth-century statesman was known as 'JFK'?

5   What does the organisation known at the RSPB look after?

6   In the story, which factory was owned by Mr Willy Wonka and had staff called Oompa-Loompas?

7   How many lines are there in a poem called a triolet?

8   What number am I thinking of if seventy-five per cent of it is three more than sixty per cent of it?

9   In the family, who would be your sororial relative?

10 In story, which American girl sleuth has two girl-friends called Bess and George?

11 What could British women do after 1928 which they couldn't do before then?

12 What particular advice does the Highway Code have for cyclists just before they start to pedal away?

ANSWERS

Game ONE   GENERAL KNOWLEDGE (1)
1 Charles Darwin.   2 K (it's worth five points, while H and V are each worth four).   3 Sandy.   4 Cheryl Baker.
5 Robin Hood.   6 A postage stamp.   7 Graffiti.   8 On coins, on the 'heads' side.   9 In the Houses of Parliament – it is the front bench Government Ministers sit on.
10 A beret!   11 Bread (or loaves).   12 Box.

Game ONE   POP MUSIC (1)
1 Dakota Building.   2 *Breaking Glass*.   3 'Star Trekkin'' sung by The Firm.   4 Johnny Logan (1980 and 1987).
5 Sting ('Russians').   6 Berlin ('Take my breath away').
7 Its twentieth anniversary.   8 The Gallup chart.
9 'Suicide is painless'.   10 Number one (in May 1980).
11 The Impostor.   12 The unemployment benefit form.

Game ONE   NEWS OF THE '80s
1 In the City of London's money markets, and the Stock Exchange. The 'Big Bang' was the name given to big changes in ways of working.   2 Canada.   3 The half pence.   4 Trades Union Congress.   5 Kenneth Baker.
6 Prince Harry (or Henry).   7 Fashion design.   8 All were victims of kidnappings.   9 Mr Kinnock, leader of the Labour Party.   10 Japan.   11 South Africa.   12 Merlin.

Game ONE   MOVIES
1 *Return of the Jedi*.   2 *Caravan of Courage*.
3 *Cinderella*.   4 John Barry.   5 The Cannes Film Festival.   6 *The Mission*.   7 *Bugsy Malone*.
8 An otter.   9 A (roaring) lion.   10 *Mary Poppins*.
11 Laurel and Hardy.   12 55.

Game ONE   SPORTS AND GAMES
1 Francis.   2 Arsenal.   3 Surrey.   4 The European Championship.   5 Athens.   6 East Germany (or the German Democratic Republic).   7 Every four years.
8 Custard pie throwing.   9 Gymnastics.   10 Marbles.
11 Canoeing.   12 Middleweight.

Game ONE   POP MUSIC (2)
1 The Flying Pickets.   2 Alan.   3 Tracy Ullman.   4 Marc
Almond.   5 M.T.V.   6 Beirut (the song was 'The
Lebanon').   7 '9 to 5' (Both had hits with a song of this
title.)   8 'Hymn'.   9 Maggie Riley.   10 The bomber which
dropped the atomic bomb on Hiroshima.   11 Nigeria.
12 Mercury (Freddie Mercury is the lead singer.)

Game ONE   GENERAL KNOWLEDGE (2)
1 Portuguese.   2 A butterfly.   3 A monkey.   4 A lizard
found in the tropics and parts of North America (1 point for
'reptile').   5 The Black Sea.   6 Australia.   7 Gross
National Product.   8 On its foot, below the fetlock.
9 Danny.   10 'My son John'.   11 None!   12 The Arctic
Circle.

Game TWO   GENERAL KNOWLEDGE (1)
1 Acts (of the Apostles).   2 Six hundred (1215–1815).
3 Kangaroo.   4 The Bolshoi.   5 Beatrix Potter.
6 To flavour food.   7 Down!   8 Russ Abbot.
9 The Pennine Way.   10 Twenty-four.   11 False –
they belong to the Arctic.   12 An Iron Age man (1 point)
whose preserved body was found in 1984 in a peat bog in
Cheshire (1 point).

Game TWO   POP MUSIC (1)
1 James.   2 *A capella*.   3 Human League.   4 Ashford
and Simpson.   5 Max Headroom.   6 Jaap Eggermont.
7 'Free as a bird'.   8 1984. 'Sexcrime (1984)' was written
for a dramatisation of Orwell's novel *1984*.   9 Colonel
Abrams.   10 Men. (Their song 'It's raining men' reached
number two.)   11 A prostitute.   12 A cocktail made from
champagne and orange juice.

Game TWO   NEWS OF THE '80s
1 June.   2 Jimmy Savile.   3 The Liberal Party.
4 Because of possible contamination after an accident at a
Russian nuclear power station.   5 1980 (on 30 June).
6 Bob Geldof.   7 Aspirin.   8 Austria.   9 An earthquake in
Mexico.   10 *The Domesday Book*.   11 Liverpool.
12 The Archbishop of Canterbury.

Game TWO   MOVIES
1 Fred Astaire.   2 John Wayne.   3 . . . *Cairo*.   4 Best
supporting actress.   5 Oscars.   6 Sydney Pollack.
7 *Lady and the Tramp*.   8 Elias.   9 *The Wizard of Oz*.
10 Bugs Bunny.   11 The 'Carry On' films.   12 Bob
Newhart.

Game TWO   SPORTS AND GAMES
1 Brown belt.   2 Derby County.   3 Boxing.   4 Seven.
5 Golf.   6 Swimming.   7 Four (it's four miles 400 yards).
8 Middleweight.   9 Nick Faldo.   10 Rugby (1 point) Union
(1 point).   11 Ice-dancing.   12 Zola Budd.

Game TWO   POP MUSIC (2)
1 *Supergran*.   2 Jan Hammer.   3 300,000.   4 Police (with
their 1980 hit 'De Do Do Do, De Da Da Da').   5 Claire.
6 Odyssey.   7 August Darnell.   8 Denise La Salle (with
'My toot toot').   9 Limahl (number four in the charts with
'Never-ending story').   10 Buck's Fizz.   11 Fun Boy
Three.   12 ZZ Top.

Game TWO   GENERAL KNOWLEDGE (2)
1 Methane.   2 Saudi Arabia.   3 Moscow (then
Manchester, then New York).   4 King's Cross, Charing
Cross.   5 Fly it – it's an old type of aeroplane.
6 The Orkney Islands.   7 The Scilly Isles.   8 Plasma.
9 Meteorology.   10 The science of measurement.
11 Turkey.   12 November (on the last Thursday of the
month).

Game THREE   GENERAL KNOWLEDGE (1)
1 Caviare.   2 Alfred, Lord Tennyson.   3 'Scarborough
Fair'.   4 King George the Sixth (must have name and
number for 2 points).   5 King George the Third (must have
name and number for 2 points).   6 In our arms (there are
thirty bones in each, compared to twenty-nine in each leg).
7 Austrian.   8 The lower part of the face. (1 point for
'head'.)   9 Iodine.   10 Ear, nose and throat.   11 Red and
amber together.   12 The Yukon Territory.

Game THREE   POP MUSIC (1)
1 Harvey Goldsmith.   2 Phil Collins (performed at both
Live Aid venues).   3 Maggie Bell.   4 'Begin the
beguine'.   5 Nick Rhodes.   6 His yacht *Drum*.
7 'Nikita'.   8 Keren, Sarah and Siobhan.   9 Nena.
10 Elkie Brooks.   11 Cliff Richard.   12 Chrissie Hynde.

Game THREE   NEWS OF THE '80s
1 Demis Roussos.   2 1982.   3 The Malvinas.   4 The
rates.   5 The newspaper industry.   6 All featured on a
special stamps issue called 'species at risk'.   7 Israel.
8 The red rose.   9 Richard Branson.   10 Balloon.
11 Pop group Wham's 'farewell' concert.   12 The Humber
Estuary.

Game THREE   MOVIES
1 James Herriot's.   2 Joan Wilder.   3 Neil Dickson.
4 Kim Basinger.   5 Butch Cassidy.   6 *Mona Lisa*.
7 *Police Academy*.   8 . . . *Tail*.   9 A skunk.   10 David
Bowie.   11 Eddie Murphy.   12 Fourteen.

Game THREE   SPORTS AND GAMES
1 Liverpool.   2 Edinburgh.   3 Two (1980 and 1984).
4 Five.   5 Swim the English Channel.   6 Cycling (CTC
stands for Cyclists' Touring Club).   7 Chess.
8 Showjumping.   9 (Downhill) skiing.   10 Aintree
Racecourse.   11 1986.   12 Steve Cram.

Game THREE   POP MUSIC (2)
1 BA Robertson ('To be or not to be').   2 Phil Collins.
3 Julio Iglesias.   4 Kate Bush.   5 Annie Mae Bullock.
6 Katrina and the Waves.   7 Berry Gordy.   8 Joan
Armatrading ('Drop the pilot').   9 Aretha Franklin.
10 'Tunnel of love'.   11 Because it showed naked girls.
12 His father.

Game THREE GENERAL KNOWLEDGE (2)
1 The triangle. 2 Queensland (second to Western Australia). 3 Round. 4 Bell-ringing. 5 Your sole. 6 True (she's the wife of Brutus). 7 Judy Blume. 8 135 degrees. 9 Jeffrey Archer. 10 Fifty. 11 Half-horse and half-human. 12 Manchester (in 1819, when cavalry charged a political meeting).

Game FOUR GENERAL KNOWLEDGE (1)
1 Phillip Schofield. 2 Belgium. 3 Doctor Who's. 4 Egypt. 5 Mountaineering. 6 Twelve. 7 *The Nutcracker* (2 points) by Tchaikovsky. 8 The day we put the clocks back after Summer Time. 9 Tuesday. 10 Crown. 11 The Caribbean. 12 A rattle-snake.

Game FOUR POP MUSIC (1)
1 'Seven and the ragged tiger'. 2 Peter Gabriel. 3 'Rock me Amadeus'. 4 Eddie Rabbitt ('I love a rainy night'). 5 Gerry Rafferty. 6 The Pretenders. 7 1959. 8 Bad News. 9 Tennant and Lowe. 10 Gary, Indiana, USA. 11 Quincy Jones. 12 Reggae.

Game FOUR NEWS OF THE '80s
1 Simon Groom. 2 Stoke on Trent. 3 Michael Foot. 4 First man to space-walk without a safety line. 5 Yugoslavia. 6 François Mitterrand. 7 St Paul's Cathedral in London. 8 Mike Smith. 9 Spain and Portugal (1 point each). 10 Wembley. 11 The Loch Ness Monster ('Nessie'). 12 To a space rendezvous with Halley's Comet.

Game FOUR MOVIES
1 *The Jewel of the Nile.* 2 Kirk Douglas. 3 Richard Chamberlain. 4 *Snow White and the Seven Dwarfs.* 5 O'Neal. 6 . . . *Beverly Hills.* 7 *Amadeus.* 8 *Chariots of Fire.* 9 The Keystone Cops. 10 Maria. 11 Lee Marvin. 12 *Paint Your Wagon.*

Game FOUR   SPORTS AND GAMES
1 Scotland and England (2 points) at football.   2 Belfast.
3 Muhammad Ali (earlier known as Cassius Clay).   4 On a
cricket field (they're fielding positions).   5 Joe Fagan.
6 Nine.   7 Horses have to jump very high fences.   8 The
front crawl.   9 Red Indians.   10 1980.   11 Moscow.
12 Sailing.

Game FOUR   POP MUSIC (2)
1 John Peel.   2 Willie Nelson (with 'To all the girls I've
loved before').   3 Pam Nester.   4 Hazel O'Connor.
5 Jim Kerr.   6 True.   7 The Heartbreakers.
8 Nikki Finn.   9 For hitting a film extra.   10 Australia.
11 Martin Luther King.   12 'Psycho candy'.

Game FOUR   GENERAL KNOWLEDGE (2)
1 Stress – the body prepares for 'fight or flight'.
2 Civilians, prisoners of war and (during wartime) wounded
soldiers.   3 Four (Yugoslavia, Austria, Switzerland and
France).   4 Betty.   5 'U'.   6 Sunday schools.   7 315
degrees.   8 Libra.   9 Benjamin.   10 Iran.   11 Mrs
Thatcher.   12 Eleven (two birds and nine stitches).

Game FIVE   GENERAL KNOWLEDGE (1)
1 An MP who wants to resign.   2 Princess Anne (to Mark
Phillips).   3 Russia and Austria.   4 Leningrad.   5 The
House of Lords.   6 Peter.   7 In a ventriloquist's act (he's
been the 'partner' of Ray Alan).   8 Clementine.   9 Cousin.
10 Thirty-three.   11 A gong (1 point for 'percussion').
12 Toronto.

Game FIVE   POP MUSIC (1)
1 It was his 100th single.   2 'Clutching at straws'.   3 Holly
Johnson.   4 'The reflex'.   5 'Life in a day' (reached
number sixty-two in November 1979).   6 'Lady Soul'.
7 St Kitts, in the West Indies.   8 Rapid Eye Movement.
9 Mike Stipe.   10 Graham Lyle.   11 Three (Andy, John,
Roger).   12 'I heard it through the grapevine'.

Game FIVE   NEWS OF THE '80s
1 The Nobel Peace Prize.   2 Dr David Owen.   3 1987.
4 Sweden.   5 Suzie Quatro.   6 *Requiem*.   7 John
Lennon.   8 Australia.   9 The wedding service of the Duke
and Duchess of York.   10 Mikhail.   11 A policy of open-
ness and frankness in government, developed after Mr
Gorbachev became leader.   12 Princess Royal.

Game FIVE   MOVIES
1 *Seven Brides for Seven Brothers*.   2 Seven.   3 Olivia
Newton-John.   4 Tarzan.   5 Sean Connery.   6 British
Academy of Film and Television Arts.   7 *La Bamba*.
8 Bob Dylan.   9 . . . *my Success*.   10 *Psycho*.   11 *Back
to the Future*.   12 A fox.

Game FIVE   SPORTS AND GAMES
1 Boxing.   2 The Commonwealth Games.   3 The
Campbells (first Sir Malcolm, then Donald and now Gina
Campbell).   4 Czech.   5 28 (15 in a rugby union team; 13
in a rugby league side).   6 Rowing.   7 Yachting.
8 Tennis.   9 Javelin.   10 1984.   11 Gary Kasparov.
12 Ian Botham.

Game FIVE   POP MUSIC (2)
1 From the villain in the film *Barbarella*, starring Jane
Fonda.   2 Johnny and the Self Abusers.   3 'Welcome to
the Pleasuredome'.   4 '19'.   5 The Pretenders.   6 'All
those years ago'.   7 'Up where we belong'.   8 Generation
X.   9 'Centrefold', 'Freeze frame' and 'Angel in blue'.
10 Peter Wolf.   11 Kingston, Ontario, Canada.   12 Tina
Turner.

Game FIVE   GENERAL KNOWLEDGE (2)
1 French.   2 Aberdeen.   3 The Disney organisation.
4 Experimental Prototype Community of Tomorrow.
5 Two.   6 Appendix.   7 John Wyclif.   8 April Fool.
9 Soft.   10 It stands on them.   11 Fifty thousand.
12 Charles Kingsley.

Game SIX   GENERAL KNOWLEDGE (1)
1 The wellington, after the Duke of Wellington.   2 Tony Hart.   3 Trade unions.   4 The Duke of Bedford.   5 Apple sauce.   6 Northern Ireland.   7 Bermuda shorts.   8 'C' (40 + 60 = 100).   9 Tangier.   10 Spain.   11 101.   12 Sarajevo in Yugoslavia.

Game SIX   POP MUSIC (1)
1 'Morning train'.   2 Philadelphia.   3 Mike Read.   4 Jeans.   5 The Vietnam War.   6 Ringo Starr and Paul McCartney.   7 Bill Medley.   8 'We've got the whole world at our feet'.   9 *Mutiny on the Bounty*.   10 1984.   11 Prince.   12 A-Ha.

Game SIX   NEWS OF THE '80s
1 None – rain washed out play.   2 Cecil Parkinson.   3 Iceland.   4 Home Secretary.   5 Argentina (after the Falklands conflict).   6 Because the cemetery, at Bitburg in Germany, included graves of Nazi SS men of World War Two.   7 To commemorate the Commonwealth Games.   8 75th.   9 Durham.   10 A three-wheeled electric car.   11 Sir Clive Sinclair.   12 The Duke of York (Prince Andrew).

Game SIX   MOVIES
1 John Cleese.   2 Young Sherlock Holmes (*Young Sherlock Holmes and the Pyramid of Fear* was the full title).   3 *Out of Africa*.   4 New York.   5 Shanghai.   6 *The Wizard of Oz*.   7 Oliver Hardy (Mr Jefferson was Stan Laurel).   8 Dumbo.   9 *The Aristocats*.   10 India.   11 Liverpool.   12 The James Bond thrillers.

Game SIX   SPORTS AND GAMES
1 The Professional Golfers' Association.   2 The West Indies.   3 Twenty-one.   4 Bantam (2 points) weight.   5 Forty.   6 Darts.   7 Fox-hunting.   8 A shuttlecock.   9 American football.   10 Seb Coe.   11 1986.   12 West Germany.

Game SIX   POP MUSIC (2)
1 Lord Olivier.   2 Jim Vallance.   3 Prince Rogers Nelson.
4 'Uptown girl'.   5 Bjorn Ulvaeus.   6 The extreme youth
of US soldiers in Vietnam.   7 Fatty 'Buster' Bloodvessel.
8 Norway.   9 Frank Dileo.   10 'The Lady in Red'.
11 Dennis Wilson.   12 Q-Tips.

Game SIX   GENERAL KNOWLEDGE (2)
1 South America.   2 Timothy the dog.   3 *The Railway
Children*.   4 Hindi.   5 Sudan.   6 They're 'scritch scritch
scratchin''.   7 Vertical.   8 Asia and North America.
9 A jacket.   10 North Yorkshire.   11 True.   12 Jupiter's.

Game SEVEN   GENERAL KNOWLEDGE (1)
1 Shrove Tuesday (or Pancake Tuesday).   2 Marie
Antoinette.   3 Mexico.   4 F (the letters are the initials of
one, two, three, four, five).   5 Long-distance solo flying.
6 Green.   7 Yugoslavia.   8 Bonn, in West Germany.
9 In the sea. (It is the sea floor under fairly shallow water
around the edge of the continents.)   10 Two (the Fifth and
Sixth).   11 The Confederation of British Industry.
12 John and Charles.

Game SEVEN   POP MUSIC (1)
1 Trevor Horn.   2 'Just for the money'.   3 'Run to you'
(number eleven in January 1985).   4 *Dirty Dancing*.
5 Kenny Rogers.   6 The Pretenders.   7 Doughnuts.
8 Elton John.   9 Southampton.   10 A fruit and vegetable
seller.   11 'Walking in the air'.   12 *Purple Rain*.

Game SEVEN   NEWS OF THE '80s
1 Victory in Europe (celebrating the Allied victory in
Europe in World War Two).   2 The Iron Lady.   3 The sale
of British Gas shares to the public.   4 Gerald Kaufman.
5 *Spycatcher*. (It was the subject of a legal battle with the
Government.)   6 1980. (He was inaugurated in 1981.)
7 Bhopal.   8 *The General Belgrano*.   9 Eric Morecambe.
10 *Starlight Express*.   11 She was the first woman to run
for vice-president of the USA.   12 By sailboard (2 points)
in 46 days.

Game SEVEN   MOVIES
1 Danny Kaye.   2 *Heavenly Pursuits*.   3 *Back to the Future*.   4 It was the first 'talking picture'.   5 Steven Spielberg.   6 Fighter pilots.   7 *Absolute Beginners*.
8 David Bowie.   9 Michael J Fox.   10 Captain W E Johns.
11 Black. (The film was *The Black Cauldron*).   12 *The Care Bears Movie*.

Game SEVEN   SPORTS AND GAMES
1 Simon Le Bon's yacht.   2 *Drum*.   3 Barcelona.
4 Steve Cram.   5 Jo Durie.   6 Highland Games (the Braemar Gathering).   7 At Wembley.   8 Snooker.
9 Mike Gatting.   10 Cram (born in 1960). Davis was born in 1957; Botham in 1955.   11 The 'three'.   12 Jockey Lester Piggott's.

Game SEVEN   POP MUSIC (2)
1 Royal Scottish Academy of Music and Drama.   2 A serious motorcycle accident on Long Island, New York.
3 Sheena Easton.   4 'When doves cry' and 'Purple rain'.
5 Douglas Trendle.   6 'A spaceman came travelling'.
7 Malcolm McLaren.   8 'C30 C60 C90'.   9 Bing Crosby.
10 'Dancing in the streets'.   11 Larry Carlton.   12 *Miami Vice*.

Game SEVEN   GENERAL KNOWLEDGE (2)
1 James.   2 Yellow or golden.   3 In England (in Northumberland).   4 Economics.   5 Rhinoceros.
6 *The Worst* (2 points) *Witch*.   7 Wednesday.   8 New Hampshire, New Jersey, New Mexico and New York States.   9 Guitar.   10 Stall.   11 Mosses.   12 On the edge of a pound coin – *decus et tutamen*.

Game EIGHT   GENERAL KNOWLEDGE (1)
1 Greece.   2 Aluminium (it makes up about 8 per cent of the earth's crust).   3 It would melt! (It melts at 86 degrees Fahrenheit.)   4 A monkey.   5 No.   6 'Scarlet Ribbons'.
7 Kansas (Kentucky is second).   8 Three – Geneva is the odd one out.   9 Africa.   10 Ten.   11 Nero . . . because both letters are near 'O'.   12 Two (1992 and 1996).

Game EIGHT   POP MUSIC (1)

1 *The Big Time.*   2 The Youth Federation of China.
3 'Human's Lib'.   4 *The Snowman* by Raymond
Briggs.   5 Rick Wakeman.   6 Ireland.   7 'No parlez'.
8 Vince Clarke and Alison (Alf) Moyet.   9 'Senses working
overtime'.   10 Tony Hadley.   11 1983.   12 *White Nights*.

Game EIGHT   NEWS OF THE '80s

1 Acquired Immune Deficiency Syndrome.   2 She became
the first woman to walk in space.   3 Sir John Betjeman.
4 Nicaragua.   5 Fashion design.   6 Michael Crawford.
7 Egypt.   8 Mrs Gandhi.   9 1983.   10 The Netherlands
(Holland).   11 Sri Lanka.   12 Six (they were the Walton
sextuplets).

Game EIGHT   MOVIES

1 Both were originally written by Ian Fleming.   2 *A Chorus
Line*.   3 . . . *Susan*.   4 South Africa.   5 An old pirate
map.   6 *Amadeus*.   7 An English public school.
8 Anthony Hopkins.   9 *Breakdance 2*.   10 *A Christmas
Carol*.   11 Two (in 1938 and 1951).   12 *The Cotton Club*.

Game EIGHT   SPORTS AND GAMES

1 Cricket.   2 Goalkeeper.   3 Seventeen.   4 Golf (You
start off at the 'tee'!).   5 Maximum Time Aloft.   6 Tennis.
7 Scotland.   8 A trainer!   9 Birmingham.
10 Barcelona.   11 Lloyd Honeghan.   12 Ice-dancer
Christopher Dean.

Game EIGHT   POP MUSIC (2)

1 Daryl Hall.   2 Boris Gardiner.   3 Linda Ronstadt.
4 Grace Slick.   5 Elvis Costello.   6 Cliff Richard.   7 Boy
George.   8 Six.   9 The two detectives from *Tin Tin* by
Hergé.   10 Cromwell's forces during the British Civil War.
11 Limahl.   12 It was only available on cassette.

Game EIGHT   GENERAL KNOWLEDGE (2)

1 The Indian Ocean.   2 Four.   3 Molars.   4 Very softly, or
quietly.   5 *EastEnders*.   6 Nearest the stern.   7 Both are
nicknames of cars.   8 Israel.   9 Four hours ('dog
watches' are two hours).   10 In the Louvre, in Paris.
11 An elephant driver.   12 Alabama.

Game NINE   GENERAL KNOWLEDGE (1)

1 A spider!   2 Fish.   3 Twenty (a nickel is five cents).
4 John Peel.   5 They vibrate their wings.   6 Kenny
Everett.   7 Sixteen centimetres.   8 One.   9 A (large,
white) bandage.   10 'U' (The yew).   11 Seven.
12 Farmers.

Game NINE   POP MUSIC (1)

1 *For your eyes only*.   2 Carol Decker.   3 Limahl's real
name, Christopher *Hamill*.   4 The Royal Family.
5 Houston, Texas, USA.   6 Diana Ross and Lionel Ritchie,
with 'Endless love'.   7 1980.   8 Meatloaf.   9 Men at
work.   10 Australia.   11 'Africa'.   12 The Toy Dolls, with
'Nellie the elephant'.

Game NINE   NEWS OF THE '80s

1 Mr Kinnock (in the election for the Labour Party
leadership).   2 A women's (1 point) peace camp (1 point)
against nuclear weapons based in Britain.   3 Jeffrey
Archer.   4 Sikh extremists were sheltering there.
5 British Rail.   6 Princess Anne.   7 Sellafield.
8 1982.   9 Henry the Eighth's flagship, the *Mary Rose*.
10 *Rainbow Warrior*, owned by the Greenpeace
conservation organisation.   11 To witness the signing of
the Channel Tunnel Treaty.   12 *Today*.

Game NINE   MOVIES

1 Bill Forsyth.   2 An ice-cream traders' war.   3 Three.
4 . . . *Broad Street*.   5 Paul McCartney.   6 *Gremlins*.
7 Two from: Shanghai, Macau and India.   8 *The Killing
Fields*.   9 Richard Burton.   10 E M Forster.   11 David
Lean.   12 *A Private Function*.

Game NINE   SPORTS AND GAMES

1 Springbok.   2 5000 metres.   3 John McEnroe.
4 Saturday.   5 Just before the race was due to begin on
the Saturday, the Cambridge boat collided with a barge
and damaged its bow.   6 Bicycle Moto Cross.   7 The
piste.   8 American football.   9 Barry McGuigan.
10 Motor racing.   11 Steve Cram.   12 The knight.

Game NINE POP MUSIC (2)

1 Best R + B male vocal performance of the year. 2 Irene Cara. 3 Was (Not Was). 4 Bono. 5 Andy Bell and Vince Clarke. 6 Victory Tour. 7 Elvis Presley. 8 *Is that it?* 9 Al Jarreau. 10 B A Robertson. 11 Wang Chung. 12 Electric Light Orchestra.

Game NINE GENERAL KNOWLEDGE (2)

1 Because they can't fly at all. 2 Hawaii, Mississippi and Missouri. 3 Maria and Yvette. 4 Tasmania. 5 Fifteen. 6 *No Place Like Home*. 7 Copenhagen (followed by Berlin and finally Vienna). 8 '. . . that is the question'. 9 Christine. 10 The holly (from 'The Holly and the Ivy'). 11 Sir Edward Elgar. 12 Round.

Game TEN GENERAL KNOWLEDGE (1)

1 'Waltzing Matilda'. 2 Nine. 3 Henry the Fifth. 4 Common Agricultural Policy. 5 The Western Pyrenees. 6 39. 7 A stethoscope. 8 Prince William. 9 The Pony Express. 10 'The Hare and the Tortoise'. 11 The Liberal Party. 12 Toast.

Game TEN POP MUSIC (1)

1 Montserrat Caballe. 2 'King of America'. 3 The Silver Bullet Band. 4 Jean Paul Goude. 5 Ian Kewley. 6 *Labyrinth*. 7 Philip Pope. 8 'Heartbreak'. 9 'Touch'. 10 David Byrne. 11 Radio One D.J. Steve Wright. 12 'So'.

Game TEN NEWS OF THE '80s

1 The plane was shot down by the Russians after it strayed into Soviet airspace. 2 The cello. 3 York Minster. 4 (Vincent) van Gogh's. 5 Buckingham Palace (an intruder managed to break into the Queen's bedroom while she was there). 6 Three (Messrs Callaghan, Foot and Kinnock). 7 The Commonwealth Games. 8 Prince Edward. 9 Paul Daniels' Show. 10 Israel. 11 It was abolished. 12 A Royal corgi.

Game TEN   MOVIES
1 Singer-songwriters.   2 Tom Conti.   3 Ford.
4 Chiropodist.   5 Colombia.   6 *The Shooting Party*.
7 She was a mermaid.   8 *Star Trek 3*.   9 *Raiders of the
Lost Ark*.   10 As Supergirl.   11 *2010*.   12 Stevie Wonder.

Game TEN   SPORTS AND GAMES
1 Epsom.   2 Cricket (it is the line in front of the wicket).
3 Mrs Ginny Leng (her maiden name was Ginny Holgate).
4 The water works and the electric company.   5 Rowing.
6 England and Australia.   7 80 (deuce is 40-40).   8 Stout
boots (a 'yomp' is a long march, made famous by the
Royal Marine Commandos during the Falklands conflict).
9 Wimbledon (the names in the question were of two
Wombles of Wimbledon and a Wimbledon tennis star).
10 Argentina.   11 Seven (four divisions in England; three
in Scotland).   12 John McEnroe.

Game TEN   POP MUSIC (2)
1 *True Stories*.   2 Noel Edmunds, Keith Chegwin and
Maggie Philbin.   3 *Top Gun*.   4 Phil Collins, Mike
Rutherford and Tony Banks.   5 'Brothers in arms'.
6 'Licence to ill'.   7 Liz Fraser.   8 Modern Talking.
9 Stryper.   10 Dexter Gordon.   11 'Smelly'.
12 'Deep in the heart of nowhere'.

Game TEN   GENERAL KNOWLEDGE (2)
1 Cauliflower.   2 Imperial Chemical Industries.   3 Yes.
4 £270.   5 Polka.   6 Joshua.   7 Vienna.   8 Queen
Victoria.   9 The Inca Empire.   10 Three (January, March
and May).   11 She stabbed him in the bath.   12 Jeans.

Game ELEVEN   GENERAL KNOWLEDGE (1)
1 Mayonnaise.   2 *Treasure Island*.   3 California.   4 The
gerbil.   5 Thumbelina.   6 Tack.   7 The rhinoceros.
8 .0001 per cent.   9 A brogue.   10 Sandhurst.   11 A
pony.   12 Eric.

Game ELEVEN   POP MUSIC (1)

1 The Attractions.   2 David Essex.   3 Fat Boys.   4 Hull.
5 Paul Weller and Mike Talbot.   6 John Coghlan.
7 Simply Red.   8 Keith Harris (with Orville).   9 Michael
Barratt.   10 'The power of love'.   11 'Mated'.   12 Lynx.

Game ELEVEN   NEWS OF THE '80s

1 Don't take drugs.   2 The USA.   3 A yacht (2 points) in
the America's Cup.   4 The ship used by explorer Scott of
the Antarctic.   5 International Youth Year.   6 No ('never
go with strangers' is the message).   7 Oxford.
8 Tommy Cooper.   9 Mark Thatcher.   10 The Berlin
Wall.   11 Prince William.   12 Elizabeth Taylor.

Game ELEVEN   MOVIES

1 *Girls* (2 points) *just want to have fun* was the title.
2 Third.   3 Danish.   4 Robert Redford.   5 . . . *Muppets*
. . . 6 Scotland.   7 Motor cycles.   8 William Shatner.
9 Jane and Michael.   10 Michael.   11 Gene Kelly.
12 Bette Midler.

Game ELEVEN   SPORTS AND GAMES

1 79 miles (78 miles, 1,155 yards precisely).
2 Wednesday (Sheffield Wednesday).   3 Motor racing.
4 Angling.   5 Everton.   6 Snooker.   7 Jack Nicklaus.
8 Mark Hughes (2 points) of Manchester United.   9 West
Tip.   10 Sarah Hardcastle (1 point) in the swimming
events (1 point).   11 Austrian.   12 Wales.

Game ELEVEN   POP MUSIC (2)

1 Nana Mouskouri.   2 Andrew Ridgeley (on his nose).
3 The Jam.   4 Drums.   5 Wham.   6 The Undertones.
7 Assembly.   8 Jon Anderson.   9 'The Gift'.   10 David
Lee Roth.   11 'Beat it'.   12 Splodgenessabounds.

Game ELEVEN   GENERAL KNOWLEDGE (2)

1 They are all important daily newspapers.   2 Snow White herself.   3 Just over four times higher – 15,771 feet compared with 3,560 feet.   4 Three (Edward the Sixth, Mary the First, Elizabeth the First).   5 They were all 'Uncles'.   6 Freezing point.   7 Coughing.   8 85 years (25 for a silver wedding and 60 for a diamond wedding). 9 Jimmy Krankie (1 point for 'The Krankies').   10 Rome. 11 Warwickshire.   12 The nineteenth century.

Game TWELVE   GENERAL KNOWLEDGE (1)

1 On food packets or tins (the numbers of additives to food).   2 Halifax.   3 'The Unready'.   4 Sculpture.   5 A foot.   6 Morocco.   7 Turkey.   8 Fifty.   9 Denis Thatcher. 10 Romantic fiction.   11 The two-acre field is bigger (four hectares is about 1.6 acres).   12 32.

Game TWELVE   POP MUSIC (1)

1 Special A.K.A.   2 Run D.M.C.   3 'Fun, love and money'. 4 Robert Smith.   5 Haysi Fantayzee.   6 Glen Hoddle and Chris Waddle.   7 They are twin brothers – Craig and Charlie Reid.   8 (Sly) Dunbar and (Robbie) Shakespear. 9 'Got my mind set on you'.   10 A station platform. 11 Status Quo.   12 The Ivor Novello Songwriter of the Year award.

Game TWELVE   NEWS OF THE '80s

1 He was an American journalist in Moscow, accused of spying but later set free.   2 The Princess of Wales (when she was shown a selection of boxer shorts on an official visit).   3 Pierre Trudeau.   4 William Golding.   5 *The Independent*.   6 633 mph.   7 Samantha Fox.   8 Leon Brittan.   9 The tobacco industry.   10 To study how the city was dealing with a large number of AIDS cases. 11 Joan Collins.   12 PW (2 points) Botha.

Game TWELVE   MOVIES

1 The Vietnam War.   2 Marx.   3 *The Never-Ending Story*. 4 New York.   5 E.T.   6 Clint Eastwood.   7 Alfred Hitchcock.   8 *101 Dalmatians*.   9 Harrison Ford. 10 Steven Spielberg.   11 Meryl Streep.   12 Three.

Game TWELVE   SPORTS AND GAMES
1 Scrambling.   2 Severiano Ballesteros.   3 Baseball.
4 The British Grand Prix, on 12 July (the Cup Final was on 16
May; the Oaks on 6 June).   5 Robin Cousins.   6 Czech.
7 Glasgow Rangers.   8 Berwick Rangers.
9 Heavyweight.   10 Tennis.   11 In the television quiz *A
Question of Sport*.   12 Bjorn Borg of Sweden, in 1980.

Game TWELVE   POP MUSIC (2)
1 'Wonderful life'.   2 Pearson.   3 An aeroplane – one of
his hobbies is flying.   4 'Respectable'.   5 'Lucille'.
6 It is Italian for 'political writing'.   7 Shalamar.
8 Gordon Sumner.   9 Bronski Beat.   10 Number ten.
11 Alexander O'Neal.   12 'Carousel waltz'.

Game TWELVE   GENERAL KNOWLEDGE (2)
1 Russian.   2 The Owl and the Pussy-Cat, in Lear's
nonsense poem.   3 One per cent.   4 Jimmy Carter
(1977-81).   5 Force Eight.   6 The budgerigar.   7 The
English Channel.   8 Little Miss Muffet (frightened by a
spider).   9 No (they were reptiles).   10 Denmark and
Norway.   11 Two (it's a kiss).   12 The three-toed sloth
(it's reckoned to be the slowest 'mover' of all land
mammals).

Game THIRTEEN   GENERAL KNOWLEDGE (1)
1 The Borrowers.   2 Hedgehogs (who've been hurt while
wandering on the roads).   3 A pig.   4 Rainfall.   5 1964.
6 Emily.   7 Peer.   8 A and D.   9 Westminster Abbey.
10 Andrew Lloyd Webber.   11 A cornet.   12 Fourteen
times.

Game THIRTEEN   POP MUSIC (1)
1 The Crusaders.   2 The Blackhearts.   3 'Sophisticated
boom boom'.   4 Don Quixote.   5 A songwriter.   6 Bass.
7 The singer Loretta Lynn.   8 From JRR Tolkien's book
The Silmarillion.   9 'Mull of Kintyre' by Wings.   10 Randy
Rhoads.   11 Four (Anita, Ruth, June and Bonnie).
12 Neil.

Game THIRTEEN   NEWS OF THE '80s

1 He was a gorilla at Jersey Zoo who tenderly cared for a small boy who fell into the gorilla enclosure.   2 Ted Hughes.   3 1983.   4 The King of Spain (2 points), King Juan Carlos.   5 Prince Andrew, Duke of York (*Brazen Hussy* was the helicopter he flew from HMS *Brazen*). 6 Southern Rhodesia.   7 The Social Democratic Party. 8 On the Thames.   9 The Philippines.   10 When a youngster invited her to play a quiz game.   11 Paris. 12 On postage stamps, or at the Post Office (a special issue featured flowers).

Game THIRTEEN   MOVIES

1 Darth Vader.   2 Julie Walters.   3 Herbert Lom. 4 Extra-Terrestrial.   5 *Superman Four*.   6 Sylvester Stallone.   7 A department store (or shop).   8 *Staying Alive*.   9 *Hearts* (2 points) *of Fire* is the film.   10 1965. 11 Foley.   12 Stanley Kubrick.

Game THIRTEEN   SPORTS AND GAMES

1 Seoul (2 points), next host of the Olympic Games. 2 Italy.   3 Shergar.   4 Golf.   5 Jimmy Connors. 6 Snooker.   7 Table tennis (or 'ping pong').   8 All are names of racehorses.   9 Judo.   10 Cricket.   11 Horse-racing (a jockey who's far in the lead can drop his hands and let the horse finish without urging).   12 Cards ('board' was an old word for 'table' – and it's hard to cheat if all the play is 'above the board'!).

Game THIRTEEN   POP MUSIC (2)

1 Nigel Planer.   2 Alan Bardon and Colin Routh. 3 'Young at heart'.   4 David Coverdale.   5 Barry Gibb. 6 The Wilsations.   7 Elvis Costello.   8 Sheila Chandra. 9 Jann Wenner.   10 Germany.   11 'Penthouse and pavement'.   12 Heads, Hands and Feet.

Game THIRTEEN   GENERAL KNOWLEDGE (2)
1 Seven.   2 South Fork.   3 The Indian Ocean.   4 White.
5 Country and Western.   6 Three (Catherine of Aragon,
Catherine Howard and Catherine Parr).   7 The cheetah.
8 A knot, said to be strong and easy to tie.   9 Edinburgh
(a school called 'St Trinnean's', whose buildings are now
part of Edinburgh University).   10 Sarah.   11 110.
12 Six (one 50, two 20, and one each of 5, 2 and 1 pence
pieces).

Game FOURTEEN   GENERAL KNOWLEDGE (1)
1 None of them.   2 590.   3 Banger.   4 Nancy.   5 Force
of earth tremors.   6 The white stripe.   7 The goldfish.
8 Mandarin.   9 Jersey (it's a breed of cattle, and the
others are ponies).   10 Twice (once in figures and once in
writing).   11 Dame Agatha Christie.   12 The seeds.

Game FOURTEEN   POP MUSIC (1)
1 Laurie Anderson.   2 Neil Arthur and Stephen Luscombe.
3 As an actor in the TV soap *General Hospital*.   4 Phil
Lynott.   5 Survivor.   6 The Who.   7 Ann.   8 Arthur
Yanoff's book *Prisoners of Pain*.   9 *The Tube*.   10 'The
tide is high'.   11 '$E=Mc^2$'.   12 Mike (Stock), Matt (Aitken)
and Pete (Waterman).

Game FOURTEEN   NEWS OF THE '80s
1 The TSB (Trustee Savings Bank).   2 The border
between Gibraltar and Spain.   3 British Caledonian
Airways.   4 To greet the Queen on her sixtieth (2 points)
birthday. (1 point for 'birthday' without the correct
age.)   5 'Young upwardly mobile' people.   6 Miss
Austria.   7 The Royal Yacht (2 points), *Britannia*.
8 1984.   9 Mr (now Sir) Ian MacGregor.   10 Geneva.
11 Defence Secretary.   12 Princess Margaret.

Game FOURTEEN   MOVIES
1 *The Great Muppet Caper.*   2 *Dirty Dancing.*   3 *Who's That Girl?*   4 Football.   5 *Pee Wee's* (2 points) *Big Adventure* is the film.   6 *On Golden Pond.*   7 Tom Cruise.
8 Gandhi.   9 *The Living Daylights.*   10 *Name of the Rose.*
11 *The Empire Strikes Back.*   12 *Hope and Glory.*

Game FOURTEEN   SPORTS AND GAMES
1 Skittles.   2 The sabre.   3 Tennis (the King says: 'We will in France, by God's grace, play a set').   4 'Gamesman-ship'.   5 Six (five plus one).   6 Virginia Wade, in 1977.
7 Cycling (or motor racing).   8 Ice hockey.   9 Royal St George's, at Sandwich (either answer gets 2 points).
10 Featherweight.   11 Mexico.   12 Amateur Athletic Association.

Game FOURTEEN   POP MUSIC (2)
1 Donald Fagen and Walter Becker.   2 'Shamrock Diaries'.   3 Philip.   4 Junior.   5 Judy Boucher.   6 Man 2 Man Meet Man Parrish (with 'Male stripper').   7 Graham Gouldman and Andrew Gold.   8 Fleetwood Mac.
9 'Dreamin''.   10 In the BBC TV series *EastEnders.*
11 The Psychedelic Furs.   12 Yawning.

Game FOURTEEN   GENERAL KNOWLEDGE (2)
1 January (April is the first with ONLY 30 days, but no points for it!).   2 The collar bone.   3 Andrew Lloyd Webber.   4 President John Fitzgerald Kennedy of the USA.   5 Birds (Royal Society for the Protection of Birds).
6 The chocolate factory (2 points) in Roald Dahl's *Charlie and the Chocolate Factory.*   7 Eight.   8 Twenty.
9 Sister.   10 Nancy Drew.   11 Vote (2 points) in parliamentary elections.   12 Look round (2 points) and make sure it's safe to move away from the kerb.